The *Constance Spry* Book of

Flower Arranging

Harold Piercy

First published in 1979 by
Sundial Publications Limited

This edition published in 1985 by
Octopus Books Limited
59 Grosvenor Street
London W1

© 1983 Text: The Constance
Spry and Cordon Bleu Group
Limited
Illustrations: Octopus Books Limited

Reprinted 1986

ISBN 0 7064 2309 7

Printed in Hong Kong

Foreword

I would like to offer my grateful thanks to all those people and organisations who have so generously given their time or their premises to help in the production of this book. Special thanks go to Olive Middleton, Fred Wilkinson and Rosemary Minter for all their help with the arrangements which appear throughout the book. Malcolm Robertson has been superb with all his help with the photographs and eye for meticulous detail. Carolyn Partridge and Joy Colesworthy were a tower of strength with their guidance in the first instance and Charlotte Mortensson and Bob Gordon have followed them and been most helpful. In fact, the whole time spent on the book was full of fun and carried out in a most enjoyable atmosphere. I am indebted to Winkfield Place for their hospitality to all the team who produced the book and visited many times and for supplying a great deal of interesting material from the garden.

Grosvenor Chapel, Holy Trinity Brompton, Cranbourne and Winkfield Parish Churches were all excellent settings for our flowers and the way in which the team was able to visit them on occasions is much appreciated. I would also like to express my gratitude to C M Watt, Esq for allowing us to photograph within his London home and to all the people who kindly loaned the use of their homes for photography.

Many thanks are due to The Constance Spry Staff, Bill 'n' Ben (textile flowers), Mr A Nolan, Mr Ashley Stephenson of the Royal Parks, Mrs Corbett of the Isle of Wight. The whole book could not have come about without the help of Pam Duck and Sue Barrett who kindly deciphered and typed my notes.

The Constance Spry
Book of
Flower
Arranging
Harold Piercy

OCTOPUS BOOKS

Contents

Introduction

There have been many books about arranging flowers and some have laid down rules and regulations to be followed, with emphasis on design, scale, balance, and harmony. No such rules are laboured here, because at the Flower School we encourage practical experience and personal taste. For instance, although much time and preparation should go into the selection of colours when arranging a group of flowers, the colour wheel should never be taken as the authority for colour combinations: flower arranging is an expression of your own sense of beauty. In this book I have tried just to be practical in my approach and pass on the tips which I have picked up over the years.

For instance, I found early on that it is wise to learn the correct names as you progress with flowers as these are universally understood. I was asked to use 'honesty' in a decoration and did so, only to discover that what I knew as honesty (*Lunaria biennis*) was not the same plant as her Ladyship wanted, and I should have used wild clematis (*Clematis vitalba*)!

I first met Constance Spry herself when once I gave a talk to an allotment association on growing flowers for cutting and she came to speak on flower arranging. At that time I knew her famous name and had one or two of her books, so I was thrilled when I found that she had been in the audience for part of my talk. She invited me to train at her Flower School and after the course I stayed to help the staff with the Coronation of Queen Elizabeth II. I must say straight away that I was only a junior and did more with a broom than with the flowers, but I was there!

The excitement of unpacking all the wonderful and unusual flowers sent from abroad was greater than any Christmas morning in my life. In those days air transport was very slow and packing flowers for transit of this kind was almost unknown. Much work had to be done to revive some of the flowers: we had coppers of water boiling so that, as they were unpacked, tired flowers were cut and their stems placed in warm water. There were hundreds of buckets in which to put the prepared blooms, which were placed on stands allotted to their country of origin, but I am quite certain that some countries accidentally got new varieties for the occasion!

When we had completed our work and everything was ready, Mrs. Spry gave us each a few leftover flowers to take home. Tears came to the eyes of my landlady as she hugged the 'Royal flowers', and all I had to arrange them in was a large pickle jar standing in a waste paper basket! I was too tired to worry, but I can still picture them in clashing red colours—a few strelitzia, roses, carnations, azaleas and some dark foliage—these were the materials left over from Westminster School Hall and a gift from the people of San Remo.

Immediately after this, the busiest week of my life, I was posted to look after the garden at Mrs. Spry's home in Berkshire. Mrs. Spry was so enthusiastic that it was a joy to work with her. She was always planning ahead and had a wonderful driving personality that kept you on your toes in the nicest way. Each year, we would be at the Chelsea Flower Show and even before it opened for the royal preview she would stand back and discuss the stand as a whole and details which she did not really think were quite right, saying, 'And next year, we must try . . .'.

A few days after I started working with her she came into the potting shed early one morning and announced that I was to go to Bournemouth that very day to demonstrate to a flower club. She wouldn't listen to my protests so I had to go. All the way down on the train I worked out what I would talk about: care and handling, containers, wire netting, etc. How could I occupy the time and not have to arrange too many vases? I had done it all before in a very simple way, but never under the Spry flag.

Since then, however, I have given demonstrations in many countries such as Japan, India and South Africa. There are so many interesting new ideas and materials coming from other countries and we can learn much from them even though they may not all follow the same technique or styles of arrangement as we do; in Japan, for example, pinholders are used on their own without any trace of wire netting and are often a visible part of the arrangement. Only a few years ago when I was in Japan demonstrating, I had the greatest difficulty obtaining any wire netting at all, and this was disastrous at the time as I rely on netting as the very foundation for my arrangements.

Experience is the best teacher of flower arranging and during my years at Spry's I have been fortunate enough to visit royal palaces and many other wonderful homes with a team of decorators. In this book I have tried to pass on the experience I have gained through years of working with flowers, but there are no rules and Mrs' Spry's words still hold good; 'Never forget that in arranging flowers you have an opportunity to express your own sense of what is beautiful and you should feel free and uninhibited in doing so'.

LEFT This striking arrangement is the result of a careful selection of a variety of materials of interesting shape and colour. In the arrangement are *Escallonia, Clematis, Passiflora caerulea, Fuchsia, Geranium, Liriope*, and the foliage of *Astrantia, Euronymus*, and *Sedum*. The arrangement is done in a small block of Oasis, fitted in a polythene bag and placed in an alabaster urn.

PAGES 4–5 A simple arrangement of the side shoots or secondary shoots of single daisy type chrysanthemums with the addition of a few pompom dahlias. Foliages used are small pieces of *Aucuba japonica*, Golden privet and ivy trails. Flowers are placed in a small piece of Oasis standing in a carved wooden dish.

PAGES 6–7 An arrangement in the making: the various plant materials, which include *Pinus, Hedera, Hyacinthus*, and *Helleborus niger*, have all received the correct stem treatment to ensure that they will last well, and are positioned one by one in the container which has been prepared with wire netting and a pinholder.

Buying and
growing flowers

Buying flowers

Naturally, flowers from a shop can be costly because of overheads but they should have received the proper treatment if the shop is a good one and this will certainly help them to last longer. Flowers keep best under cool airtight conditions, so those offered by a street trader may often have deteriorated after a day or so exposed to the cold or heat and perhaps a drying wind.

Always look at the foliage on cut flower stems and at the base of the stems, as discolouration indicates age and the smell will certainly give you an idea of the length of time that they have been standing in water.

Here are a few specific tips which may be helpful when buying flowers.

Iris, tulips, gladioli and daffodils should be bought when in bud, with the flower colour just showing. They will soon open in a warm place. Fresh daffodils once opened should make a rustling sound when shaken —those past their best will have soft petals which no longer make a sound and appear papery. Gladioli should have just the first flower open at the base of the spike. Some people recommend taking out the tip, which may help the other flowers to open right to the top.

Single daisy type flowers, for example all year round chrysanthemums (sometimes known as American spray chrysanthemums), should have a hard green centre with just a small ring of pollen showing yellow at the base of the petals: a raised centre disc of yellow (covered in pollen) means that flowering is nearly over.

Roses should always be bought as nicely shaped fat buds with good foliage right up the stem. Some varieties are much better than others at keeping their shape.

Mimosa should always be purchased from a polythene pack and never from outside in the open air: its pollen dries in the open air and sheds more quickly. Always look at it carefully to see that the small fluffy flowers which go together to make the compound spikes are just opening, and then it should last a little while.

Poppies should be showing only a trace of colour as the bud scales split because they open very quickly once in water.

As flowers are much more expensive than they used to be, many florists will sell individual flowers rather than bunches and so you can often buy the exact number that you need for an arrangement. Some florists will sell mixed bunches.

Many flowers are available for most of the year. Heaths and rhododendrons are a good example. Camellias start in January and go through to July, and hellebores go from November until July. Some glasshouse and outdoor crops have no specific season. Chrysanthemums are available all the year round, although they are much more prolific during certain months. Border carnations and anemones are available most of the year, and freesias are now joining them. Flowers will be cheapest in their natural season; if you require flowers out of their normal season, they will have been imported from abroad so there will be extra costs. Anything 'forced' to make it appear earlier than it would normally be available on the market will also be more expensive. With modern growing techniques, and rapid transport facilities, there is nothing that cannot be produced if you are prepared to pay the cost.

There is an unfortunate modern tendency for an increasing number of flowers to be dyed; I consider this to be a great pity, for there are so many beautiful flowers available in natural colours. Dyeing has been introduced by the commercial growers who produce one prolific crop of white flowers and colour them to suit demand. Some are extremely well done, but a dyed flower should never be used if a natural alternative is available.

The commercial market seldom caters for pretty foliages, and the flower arranger who has only a small garden, with little room to grow extra flowers for cutting, may find it helpful to grow some useful foliages to use with bought flowers for indoor arrangements.

PAGES 10–11 The Constance Spry flower shop in London.
BELOW Wild parsley and grasses placed in a beer mug make a simple decoration.

Wild flowers

Many wild flowers can be used very successfully in flower arrangements but there is
now a law to protect wild plants from indis-
criminate picking and virtually every species
in this country (with the exception of a few
poisonous weeds) has some measure of
protection.

It is an offence for anyone to dig up a wild
plant (including flowering plants, ferns,
mosses, liverworts and lichens) without the
permission of the owner or occupier of the
land on which it grows.

Flowers and fruits can still be picked from
wild plants but, since many countryside
plants have become quite scarce, it is very
important to pick with the greatest care,
taking only from plants common in the
locality and cutting very few pieces from
each plant. If you find just a small group of
something that attracts you, remove only
one or two pieces and never take everything.

There are, however, twenty-one plants
which are so rare that even picking would
be harmful to them, and these plants, illustrated overleaf, are totally protected. Removal of any part of these plants is an
offence under the *Conservation of Wild
Creatures and Wild Plants Act 1975*. Copies
of the Act may be obtained from HMSO book-
shops.

When travelling in the countryside, it is
useful to take a large polythene bag, a pair
of scissors and a newspaper. If you cut anything, damp the newspaper and lay it carefully in the base of the polythene bag and
then place the cut materials onto the paper
as quickly and carefully as possible. Seal up
the bag and keep it in a cool place until the
materials can be sorted out and treated in
the correct way. All flowers last best if kept
cool and airtight.

ABOVE This
arrangement in a
small basket shows
what can be done
with a few flowers
carefully picked
from a country lane.

Protected wild plants

MEZEREON
Daphne mezereum

RED HELLEBORINE
*Cephalanthera
rubra*

WILD GLADIOLUS
Gladiolus illyricus

OBLONG WOODSIA
Woodsia ilvensis

SPIKED SPEEDWELL
Veronica spicata

SNOWDON
LILY
Lloydia serotina

ALPINE WOODSIA
Woodsia alpina

DIAPENSIA
Diapensia lapponica

DROOPING
SAXIFRAGE
Saxifraga cernua

CHEDDAR PINK
Dianthus gratianopolitanus

ALPINE SOW-THISTLE
Cicerbita alpina

KILLARNEY FERN
Trichomanes speciosum

MILITARY ORCHID
Orchis militaris

MONKEY ORCHID
Orchis simia

DY'S-SLIPPER
*Cypripedium
calceolus*

GHOST ORCHID
*Epipogium
aphyllum*

TEESDALE
SANDWORT
Minuartia stricta

TUFTED SAXIFRAGE
Saxifraga cespitosa

SPRING GENTIAN
Gentiana verna

BLUE HEATH
Phyllodoce caerulea

ALPINE GENTIAN
Gentiana nivalis

15

The flower arranger's garden

Half the fun of arranging flowers is in growing them for yourself. Mrs. Spry was a wonderful gardener and had a great knowledge of plants. If you are a good grower, you will usually find your tender care of the plants well rewarded by their longer life in your arrangement. Many students come to the Flower School after studying horticulture and it is quite noticeable how well they handle their materials as a result of knowing how much care has gone into producing the flowers and foliages. Similarly, many flower arrangers, having come to know and love the plants they use, develop an interest in growing their own materials.

Planning the garden

Personal taste plays a big part in what you grow; some people will go for a lot of colour, others may prefer shape and texture and be happy with only mixed green foliages. Whatever your preference, choose plants with your room colourings in mind and grow only the varieties or colours that will be of use to you when decorating.

If the garden is large enough it is a good idea to grow some plants solely for garden decoration and to have others in nursery rows for cutting purposes only, but in many cases there will not be enough room to grow all the materials required so very careful planning will be necessary.

If only a small space is available it may make sense to grow mostly foliage plants and shrubs and to buy the cut flowers from your local florist. Such a garden would also be labour-saving because once the plants are established they will need little attention. Evergreen shrubs, silver-grey foliages, and plants giving not only flowers but also Autumn colour and perhaps berries, are well worth considering for the small garden.

A walled garden is a great asset and can offer an extra source for cutting materials. For example, some of the old-fashioned climbing roses such as 'La Follette' would be suitable. The rose 'Constance Spry' flourishes as a free-growing rose in the border but with limited space it is worth trying against a wall. Clematis, passion flower, cobaea and ivies would also be excellent.

When planning the garden, remember to allow plants plenty of room to develop. Use mostly perennial plants and add interesting annuals, biennials and bulbs when space is available: this will allow the maximum amount of variety and the longest flowering period possible. A small heated greenhouse will greatly extend the growing season.

A little pruning may be necessary to keep the plants in good shape and the trimmings can be used in arrangements, but however much you may require certain pieces, be fair to the plant and do not over-prune as this will spoil its natural habit. The plant must have first priority! Always cut (never tug) to a growing point, and do not leave snags of wood to die back.

The positioning of each group of plants in the garden needs a great amount of care and the same rules should be observed here as for a flower arrangement. Try to keep different shaped foliages and colours next to each other, allowing for variation in height and bearing in mind the ultimate size to which the plant will grow. Poor planning and planting in the garden will worry the discerning eye just as much as incorrect placement of stems in a flower arrangement and, of course, it will be far more difficult to remedy without uprooting the plants.

RIGHT AND BELOW Interesting foliages are essential for flower arrangement and are well worth growing to supplement flowers bought from a florist. These pictures show the author's small city garden in Spring (right) with a planted trough in the foreground, and Autumn (below.)

Cutting garden flowers

BELOW Another view of the author's small foliage garden in Autumn looking down on *Hebe, Azalea, Ruta, Laurus nobilis* and *Helleborus*, with a background of *Hedera*. See previous page.

When cutting flowers from the garden, carry a bucket of water with you and immediately each stem is cut, place it in the bucket. Do not leave it to dry out while gathering other flowers and never leave flowers in heaps on the ground to be collected at a later time. Wait until everything is gathered in the house or garden shed before grading it into stem categories for special treatment.

Always use a good pair of secateurs or scissors when cutting. Make a clean cut and never tug at the material or you may loosen the plant and cause it to die. Judicious pick-ing is a matter of great importance and no single plant should be cut too heavily, except annuals or biennials grown specifically for cutting. In fact, it is essential to keep cutting annuals if they are to flower over a long season. Once they have set seed, their life cycle is completed and they will stop flowering.

Much is said about not cutting flowers in the heat of the day. Commercial growers cut flowers at all hours until the crop is harvested, but I prefer to cut either in the early morning or the early evening, allowing the flowers to stand in a bucket of water and drink for a whole day or night before arranging them.

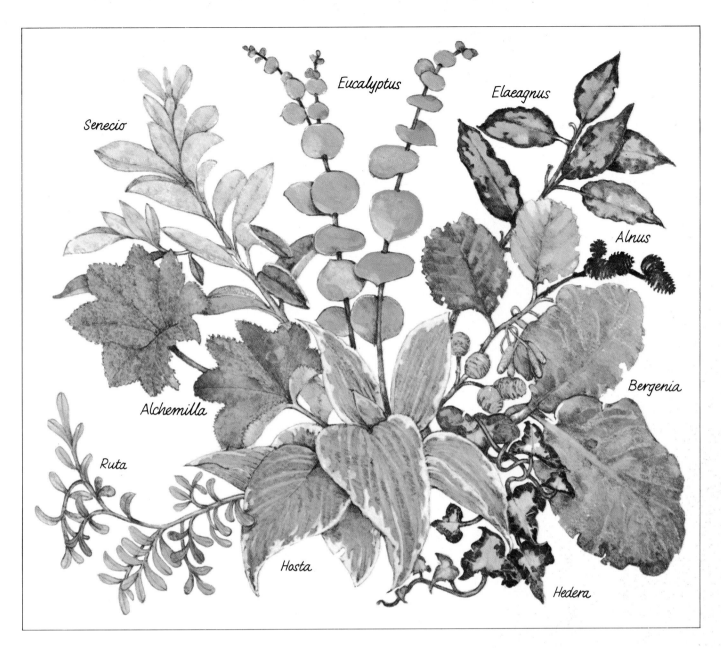

Senecio · Eucalyptus · Elaeagnus · Alnus · Bergenia · Alchemilla · Ruta · Hosta · Hedera

Foliages for the garden

Most of the materials listed below are not usually available from a florist and are well worth growing in the garden. Additional information is given at the end of this book about all these and other useful plants for the flower arranger, many of which can also be grown very successfully in the garden. Some plants, however, can be difficult to grow in certain soils without a lot of extra soil preparation and are quite costly to maintain over the years, so it is always wise to check with a reliable gardening authority before sowing or planting.

Acer
Alchemilla
Alnus glutinosa
Aralia elata
Arbutus unedo

Artemisia
Arum italicum
  pictum
Arundinaria
Aucuba japonica

Berberis
Bergenia
Betula
Bocconia cordata
Buxus
Camellia
Carpinus betulus
Cedrus
Cineraria maritima
Cornus mas
Corylopsis pauciflora
Corylus avellana
Cynara scolymus
Cytisus
Elaeagnus
Escallonia
Eucalyptus
Euonymus
Euphorbia
  epithymoides and
  E. wulfenii

Fagus
Foeniculum vulgare
Geranium
Hedera
Hosta
Ilex aquifolium
Lamium
Larix
Ligustrum
  ovalifolium 'Aureo
  Marginata'
Lonicera
Mahonia
Onopordon
Osmanthus
Paeonia
Phalaris
  arundinacea
Phormium tenax
Pieris
Polygonatum

Prunus
Pulmonaria
Pyracantha
Rhododendron
Ribes sanguineum
Rosmarinus
Ruta
Salix
Salvia
Santolina
Senecio laxifolius
Smilacina
Sorbus aria
  'Lutescens'
Spiraea
Stachys lanata
Symphoricarpos
Typha
Verbascum
Viburnum lantana
Vitis

The care of cut flowers

ABOVE This attractive arrangement in pink colourings includes a number of materials which require special stem treatment before arrangement. The woody stems of *Syringa, Sorbus aria lutescens*, and *Rhododendron* are hammered, and the *Tulipa* are wrapped in paper during their first drink. All leaves are removed from *Syringa* stems, and those of *Rhododendron* have been thinned to allow the flowers to show to good advantage. The main foliage in the arrangement comes from *Eucalyptus* and *Hosta*.

PAGES 20–1 A trug basket of flowers ready for stem treatment: soft stems are cut at an angle and woody stems are cut and hammered.

What is understood by the terms 'life of cut flowers' and 'lasting well'? A good example is the garden rose: if we pick it in bud and find that it gradually opens up in water, until it is full blown and the petals begin to fall from the stem, we know that we have seen it at its best. Even on the bush in the garden it would probably not have had a longer life. Conversely, if the rose droops while still in bud and gradually shrivels, this indicates that we have not treated it properly and that it has suffered a premature death.

The lasting qualities of flowers and foliages once cut vary considerably, but a lot can be done to extend their life by a few days, and it is well worth all the effort. It is very sad to think of the time and care that goes into producing a crop of flowers being wasted because of a little lack of attention to the cut stems.

The correct stage at which the flowers are cut is very important and the time between cutting and placing in water plays a large part in keeping certain flowers alive. Flowers picked when fully open cannot be expected to last as long as buds which are just opening. On the other hand, if a flower is picked too early, it will never develop into its true full-sized bloom.

A collection of containers ranging from a deep bucket to a shallow dish will be needed. Some flowers should have a long drink in fairly shallow water (daffodils and narcissi, for example), others such as anemones and hellebores require saturating in deep water before being used. All containers should be thoroughly cleaned before being used. Fresh water from the tap is best for all flowers and the temperature may be varied according to the specific needs of the plant material. Water collected in water butts or from a pond in the garden should not be used as it is teeming with bacteria which will readily breed in the warm conditions inside the house. Bacteria make the water smell unpleasant and block the stem vascular tissue which will result in poor water absorption and so greatly reduce the life of the flowers. The addition of chemicals to the water extends the life of some flowers and is worth considering, especially for showing. Chrysal, a popular proprietary substance which has been introduced from Holland, is a plant food which contains a stimulant and disinfectant. It should be used strictly according to instructions. It will make materials last a few days longer and flowers grow and develop well when arranged in it.

The main points for the care of cut flowers and foliage are:

Put materials into water as soon as possible after cutting.

Always use clean water.

Stand materials in a cool place to have a long drink, preferably overnight, before arranging.

Anything which has wilted should go into really warm water.

Spray overhead with a fine mist of water to charge the air with moisture.

No foliage should remain on any stem which when arranged will be below the water line.

All flowers should have their stems cut at an angle so that if they should slip to the bottom of a dirty container the stem cannot fall flat on the base and perhaps stop the intake of moisture.

Remove any broken stems or leaves, and thin out unwanted shoots.

Flowers and foliages can be brought forward a little after cutting by being placed in warm water in a warm place, adding more warm water as necessary. Keep the atmosphere around them very moist by spraying continually with a fine mist of water to create a feeling of April showers and soften the bud scales, enabling them to open more readily. Never attempt to open flowers with your fingers or mechanical aids; you will bruise the delicate, immature flower petals and as they open they will be badly marked.

Most cut flowers cannot stand hot dry air for long. It soon robs them of their natural moisture and causes them to wilt and die. They should be protected from the direct rays of hot sunshine. In heated rooms the most that can be done is to see that the flowers are not subjected to direct heat. Place them as far away as possible from heat sources and pay special attention to keeping

RIGHT This is a 'collection' of flowers rather than an arrangement in the true sense, since, having so many different materials in the group, the stems have a stuffed appearance and do not appear to radiate well from the beautiful bronze urn in which they are placed. In the arrangement are *Galtonia, Gladiolus, Crinum, Hydrangea, Amaranthus caudatus* 'Viridis', *Phytolacca, Helianthus, Dahlia, Symphoricarpos, Kniphofia, Acanthus mollis, Passiflora, Solidago, Nicotiana, Humulus*, and *Bergenia* leaves.

the vases topped up with water.

Draughts can kill flowers, too, especially those which have been brought in from the moist warm air of the glasshouse.

Certain flowers drink a surprising amount of water during the first few hours after arrangement. The vase should be filled up to the brim when the arrangement is finished and should be topped up with warm water within a few hours if necessary. There is no need to change the water in an arrangement if all leaves have been kept away from the water level and if clean stems and a clean vase were used.

Whether they have been bought from a flower shop or picked from the garden, all flowers and foliages should be properly treated before being arranged in a vase. There are particular treatments for each stem group and different soils and methods of cultivation also have a bearing on the way in which garden flowers should be treated. Flowers that do not respond to one

treatment may well benefit from another, and the best method is found by trial and error. Only by constant observation and experiment do we become aware of how flowers respond to the different treatments.

The great interest in flower arrangement shown by so many people today has resulted in many useful discoveries and recommendations for making flowers last, although often these have no scientific background. It is certainly no old wives' tale that flowers last well in metal containers and that aspirin helps to keep flowers fresh; the aspirin slows down the breeding rate of the bacteria and so helps the plant material to take up water. A copper penny in the water gives off a trace of copper which acts on the bacteria in the same way. A few drops of weak disinfectant in the water will also keep it sweet-smelling. Never dismiss a suggestion without first trying it; it may well help, and all the suggested treatments have resulted from experiments in the first instance.

BELOW Stem treatments. From left to right: stems of *Viburnum opulus sterile* are woody and should be hammered. The first stem has most of its foliage removed, the second shows the same shrub, less well developed with green flowers. *Syringa vulgaris* (centre) should have all its foliage removed, and the outer thick bark should be cut away to the white cambium layer. *Scilla nutans* has a soft stem which should be cut at an angle and placed in warm water. *Tulipa* have soft stems and because of their heavy heads they need wrapping in paper while having their first long drink. It is usual to roll stems in groups of five or ten.

Hard woody stems

Many useful flowers and foliages fit into this group. All the main trees, shrubs and blossoms—apple, cherry and plum, for example—come into this class, together with stocks, outdoor chrysanthemum and wallflowers. These stems should be cut at an angle and, if they are very woody, an inch of bark should be removed from their base so that the cambium layer (the white stem beneath the bark) shows clearly. The stem is then split with a strong pair of secateurs, or hammered to break up the fibres. Any foliage that would appear below the water level should be cut off and any damaged or unwanted shoots trimmed out before the stem is placed in a bucket of deep water. If there has been a time lag between cutting the branches of foliage and getting them into water, it is a good idea to place the tips in really hot water for a few minutes immediately before standing them in warm water for a long drink.

Lilac comes in two very different forms. The forced Dutch lilac, which is with us during December to the end of March, has very long straight stems with little or no foliage and a large flower head at the top. The main colour is white, but a little mauve is often available. These stems should be hammered and placed in very hot water for a long drink. If the flowers wilt they should be sprayed with a fine mist of cold water, and their stems should be re-cut, put in hot water and left to stand in a cool place for a few hours. If bought in good condition, forced lilac can last up to ten days. It is an ideal flower to have for a large group in early Spring.

Garden lilac in its many colours, picked during May and June, is full of leaf and this presents a problem. The stems are not usually straight and often carry a number of flower heads and many clusters of leaves. The stems cannot support this burden and the flower heads at the tips of the stems wilt due to insufficient water reaching them. The solution is to remove all the leaves and short foliage shoots from the flowering stems, and arrange the shoots separately among the flowering stems in the vase. The woody stems are treated in exactly the same way as the forced lilac.

Soft stems

This group of materials have soft succulent stems; examples are arum lilies and clivia. Their stems should be cut at an angle and placed straight away in deep water. Hyacinths and narcissi, which also come into this class, both exude a slimy sap which can damage other flowers. They should be cut and placed in water on their own until the sap has seeped from the cut stem, a matter of an hour or so, and then put into fresh clean water, when they will be ready to arrange as you choose.

Tulips should have their soft stems cut cleanly at an angle and if they are rather thick split them for 1 cm ($\frac{1}{2}$ inch). Remove the bottom leaves and place all the heads level, rolling bunches of ten or so stems together in stiff 'wet-wrapping' paper (a type of greaseproof paper), just covering the flower heads to keep them in an upright position. This will stop the flower heads from falling forward and breaking off. Place them in a deep container of tepid water for a long drink before removing the paper. Some people suggest feeding tulips with a sugar solution but I find this unnecessary. Once arranged they should take up graceful curves and continue to grow. Arrange tulips one or two days before they are wanted to give them time to take up their curves.

Lily-of-the-valley is available in a forced form during most of the year but because it is very costly to produce, I seldom use it except for special occasions. It is sold attached to its pencil-thick roots which are wrapped in newspaper, and these should be cut off straight away. The tips of the cut stems are then lightly crushed and placed in warm water in a cool place for a few hours. Forced lily-of-the-valley has very pale green foliage, long fragile stems with bells more widely spaced than those from the garden, and a very delicate scent. It has quite good lasting qualities. The lily-of-the-valley from the garden is available from May to July, depending on which part of the country it grows in. It has shorter, more woody stems

with many more bells, dark green foliage and a much stronger scent. Unfortunately it does not last long, but to prolong its life as much as possible crush the stems and place them in warm water.

Hollow-stemmed flowers

Examples of these are large delphiniums, lupins, hollyhock and large dahlias. Their life will be extended a little if immediately after cutting they are inverted and their hollow stems filled with warm water from a small can and plugged with cotton wool before being returned to the bucket.

Amaryllis comes into this group, but needs even more care. The flower head is often so heavy that it will snap off just at the neck of the stem. A piece of split bamboo cane placed in the centre of the stem will give it the necessary support, but be careful not to puncture the stem with the cane. Fill the supported stem with water and plug it with cotton wool. It may also be helpful to place an elastic band around the base of the stem to stop it splitting and curling up.

Stems which bleed

Euphorbias and poppies belong to this group. Dandelions are an example of stems which bleed; when they are picked a white ring of thick, milky sap forms at the cut surface. You can either singe the cut tip of the stem in a candle flame for a few seconds or place

BELOW Stem treatments. From left to right: a stem of *Helleborus foetidus* which has started to go to seed. At this stage of development these stems take water well and just require a clean slanting cut. *Amaryllis* stems should be supported with a thin stick, then filled with water and plugged with cotton wool. *Euphorbia palustris* is a stem which bleeds and the cut stem tip must be sealed with a flame or boiling water before being placed in warm water.

the tips in shallow boiling water for thirty seconds, taking care to protect the rest of the stem from the steam. The poinsettia, which is a euphorbia, poses an extra problem; if any leaf is removed during arranging, the scar should be sealed by a candle flame.

Hellebores are really valuable flowers for the arranger. Flower colours are from pure white to pinks, mauves and dark purple and a fine range of pale greens. *Helleborus foetidus* is a very useful hellebore and can be cut from February to the end of June. The other forms start in November and go through to May.

Hellebores last well while growing in the garden but as they like moisture and coolness it takes a time to acclimatize them to room temperatures. Always place hellebores in warm water immediately after cutting. The stem length will vary considerably with season and variety but should never be allowed to dry out. Some people recommend putting pin pricks right up the stem to the flower head; others make a razor cut straight up the stem; and some arrangers make a small hole right through the stem just below the flower head. These treatments help young flowers to take up water, but once the seed pods have formed and the stem tissue has matured, no such treatment will be necessary. All hellebores should have the extreme tips of their stems placed in boiling water for thirty seconds, with the heads

protected from the steam. Then give them a long drink in deep warm water, allowing it to cool naturally, and cut away the damaged stem tip before arranging. It is always important to arrange these flowers with their stems fully immersed in water, and when they show signs of wilting to treat them as before with hot water. Unfortunately, the more beautiful the flower, the more quickly it is likely to go down.

Roses call for special treatment, particularly the long-stemmed ones from the florist. The length of the stem controls the price of the rose, so it is hard to understand why long-stemmed roses are so popular, as most roses do not last well if left at their full length. Also, the stems are often so long that the arranger has no container in which to place them and is forced to cut them shorter!

Unless one is to be used as a specimen in a single rose container, roses should have all their thorns removed, either by rubbing (running the back of a closed pair of scissors along the stem) or by cutting them from the stem. Any excess foliage should also be removed straight away. Garden roses seldom wilt when cut and may be placed in deep water immediately after cutting. If they are at all limp, glasshouse roses should be wrapped in a roll of stiff paper and given a long drink prior to arranging. As the flower head is at the point farthest away from the

BELOW Stem treatments. From left to right: *Hydrangea* flowers will only last as cut flowers if borne on one- or two-year old wood. The darker colour of the second-year wood shows up clearly here. *Rosa* should be dethorned and have unnecessary foliage removed.

Special treatments

Mimosa How often does one hear people say 'I don't use mimosa because it doesn't last'? Unfortunately, this is very true when it is arranged in a warm dry room. Mimosa is only fluffy when the flowers are fully out and covered with pollen, towards the end of the life of the flower. Once the pollen is shed, fertilization takes place, and the flower dies at the expense of a developing seed capsule.

It is necessary to retard the development of the pollen and this can be done by keeping the stems of mimosa in a polythene bag in a damp cool place. Once arranged, it should be kept as cool as possible. It is best to make one large arrangement of it for a special occasion (never mix it with other flowers) and enjoy it for the short time you have it. If using it for a party decoration, always leave its arrangement until just before it is required to see it at its best. Never use mimosa in table decorations because its smell will taint food very quickly.

Violets Unfortunately, the day of the lovely scented violet has nearly passed, and we no longer receive those that used to come from the south of France. The short Herrick violet, very dark in colour and scentless, is our main variety nowadays but even this is less common.

Violets absorb water through their heads so it is important always to keep moisture around them. Always arrange them in little clumps and keep the heads wet by immersing them in water for a short period each day. They look best in little moss gardens or tucked down deep among other Spring flowers as a table centrepiece.

Hydrangea This is usually used as a pot plant in the early part of the Summer and cut from the bush in the latter part of the year. It is important to see that the flower head is borne on one- or two-year-old wood (stems of pencil thickness) because the older, thicker branches will not take up water properly. Hydrangeas can be placed under water for a few hours to be really charged with moisture before use in an arrangement. If the flower has been forced it tends to be very soft and it will not stand up as a cut flower in a warm room, so it is better to remove some of the soil from a pot plant, pack the ball of roots in damp moss in a polythene bag, and place this in the centre of the flower group to get the effect of cut stems. In the latter part of the year, hydrangeas will dry naturally in a vase.

Sweet peas The petals go papery if allowed to remain wet so only spray them very lightly overhead. Cut the stems at an angle and place them in deep water for a long drink before arranging them.

ABOVE Decorative cabbage. Wrap smelly stems such as this in cotton wool treated with disinfectant and place them in a polythene bag before putting them in an arrangement.

water, it is the first to wilt, and if this happens it may crack the stem tissue making it impossible to straighten the stem and revive the flower. At the first sign of wilting, the wrapping treatment must be carried out again. Recut the stems and split them, place the tips in boiling water for thirty seconds, then wrap the stems and flowers in stiff paper and give them a long drink in lukewarm water. Alternatively, recut the stems and submerge the whole flower and stem in a bath of water for a couple of hours, then place them in deep water in a cool place.

Some roses are much longer lasting than others. The old-fashioned roses, such as 'Madame Pierre Oger' and 'Cardinal de Richelieu', which are so much in demand these days, tend to be short lived but carry so many buds that when one flower goes over, another often manages to take its place, thus extending its decorative life.

Smelly stems

Flowers or foliages which are known to smell when arranged in water, such as a large stem of decorative cabbage, are best used with the cut stem isolated from the water in the vase. Wrap the stem in a pad of wet cotton wool treated with a disinfectant and place it in a small polythene bag.

Containers

ABOVE A clear glass basket holds the delicate stems of *Convallaria majalis* with its own foliage and a few of the first flowers of the small climbing rose 'Cecile Brunner'. Note how the roses have been brought through the arrangement, keeping the open (heavier) flowers in the centre.

PAGES 28–9 A variety of containers, including some which were not specifically designed for flowers but can be useful such as the sea shell, fruit dish and glass goblet.

The main purpose of arranging flowers is to see that they are presented in the most satisfactory and effective way possible. Great care must be given to shape, proportion and colour and there must be compatibility between the vase and flowers. The shape and height of the vase plays an important part in achieving the correct final result; top-heavy arrangements, groups that are too squat or skimpy, delicate flowers in too overpowering a vase or heavy flowers in a delicate one, will all offend the discerning eye.

On occasions the vase may be almost as important as the flowers themselves, particularly when you have just a few flowers to be arranged elegantly. There are times, however, when the vase serves solely as a container for water in which the flowers are anchored—even a baking tin can take an arrangement if it is concealed by the flowers or foliage.

To a certain extent, fashion dictates the use of some vases. The épergne and silver trumpet vase have had their turn and are seldom seen today, but that does not mean they will not come back. Many of us wish that the vases of our grandparents' day had been saved for our use; they would often solve the problem of the right vase for the occasion!

Glass

Many modern glass vases are designed to be ornaments and in no way are they really safe to use for flower arrangements. I look with horror at some of the designs I see on sale. If you are choosing glass, aim at a shape such as a basket, short-stemmed chalice or tazza which has a firm and heavy base and room to hide the netting under the flowers so that a confusion of stems and netting does not spoil the finished picture.

Glass must be kept perfectly clean and polished and always washed with soap and water immediately after use. A watermark easily occurs and this must be removed regularly otherwise it will become permanent. A piece of lemon dipped in salt and rubbed round the rim will help to remove stains. Bleach and disinfectants are also useful. As a last resort you can use a little hydrochloric acid for really badly marked glass, although this must be done with great care under the chemist's instruction and rubber gloves must be worn.

Probably the least useful glass vase is the cut glass vase or fruit bowl. The true beauty of cut glass is only seen when the light passes through it and produces excellent colour reflections; when filled with flowers the reflections are lost. Many of the vase

shapes found in cut glass could easily be replaced with ordinary pottery vases, which would hold the flowers in exactly the same way without creating the problem of hiding the wire netting and flower stems.

Old-fashioned milk glass or a really beautiful clear goblet both look enchanting for well arranged flowers, and for the centre-piece of a modern table setting, one of the brandy-type glasses from the Scandinavian countries could look superb holding a floating open rose. A modern shallow glass on a long stem looks excellent for a small party with a candle in the centre and the flowers high above the table to be well away from the food. One flower ideally suited to a balloon glass is the violet: a bunch of violets, lightly tied, resting in the centre of the glass base makes a very pretty setting and they will last much longer in the moist atmosphere of the glass interior.

The glass specimen vase excellently displays the beauty of a single rose. Unfortunately many of these vases are so badly designed that they easily topple over when, for example, the rose opens its petals. Choose a sensible design which has a firm solid base and is not too tall. The rose stem in a specimen vase should retain its thorns because these produce the bubbles which are attractive magnified by the glass.

Marble and alabaster

Marble has the advantage of being very heavy, so over-balancing will not be a problem. Alabaster is not so heavy and is far more fragile. Both are sought after by flower arrangers and are now fairly rare to find and very expensive. The bigger vases are often put together with glue and care must be taken not to get the joints wet because they could soften and fall apart. Always provide waterproof linings for such vases. Remember, too, that water roughens the surface of alabaster vases after a time and heat causes it to lose its translucence and makes it opaque, so do not let a good tazza stand in the window in full sun for weeks on end. Wipe over alabaster vases with a good quality olive oil from time to time as this will help to keep them in good condition.

Imitation marble and soapstone
There are a few very good cherub-type vases and chalices made from a composition which really does resemble the valuable marble and soapstone carved vases; it is heavier than plastic and the vases are normally quite well balanced. Careful selection and choice of colour will reward you with a very useful vase which may be suitable for a wide range of materials.

ABOVE Five 'Golden Rain' roses at different stages of their development arranged in a heavy crystal pot.
ABOVE LEFT a good design of specimen vase holding two 'Paul's Scarlet' rose stems.

31

China vases

Simplicity of shape is important for all containers and a plain colour is much easier to use than one which is gaily ornamented or highly coloured as these will restrict the materials which may be used.

Some coloured vases can only be used for certain flowers: I have in mind a glorious little black vase of mine with beautiful china auricula flowers modelled on its sides. It is just right when auriculas can be used to fill it but when their short season of flowering is over other flowers look quite wrong in it.

Antique white china vases, with a painting of a mixed bunch of flowers, are lovely filled with simple mixed flowers which pick up the colours on the vase. If the vase has a scalloped edge care must be taken when moving it, otherwise it will readily allow a flow of water down the side! There are modern equivalents but they are often a poor shape and badly painted and look unsightly when filled with flowers.

If one has room for only a few vases, keep to the simple shapes and plain coloured ones —black, white, celadon green, grey and pewter colourings are the safest, as bright colours can be difficult to use.

ABOVE This dolphin vase holds a small block of Oasis in which some interesting flowers are placed. The tall flowers at the back are *Lilium martagon album*, *Hoya carnosa* are the large, almost artificial-looking pink flowers in front, and sprays of wild strawberries flow over on the right. Other foliages in the arrangement are variegated ivy and ivy-leafed *Geranium* 'Sussex Lace'.
LEFT Three amusing cupid-type vases.

Cupids

The cupid-type vases are very popular and over the last ten years have appeared in many shapes and sizes. The Victorian ones, which can be expensive, are fine figures but some modern ones can also be very good. Cupid vases can take all types of flowers but they must be in proportion to the size of the vase. Cherubs labouring under great weights spoil the whole picture. I often smile when I hear a prospective purchaser in the flower shop saying, 'Have you got a good-looking boy?', but they are quite right; some seem quite cherubic from a distance but on close inspection the little faces look quite dis-gruntled! Perhaps they are worried about the weight they may have to carry!

Many cupid vases have scalloped edges, and care must be taken when filling and moving these vases as it is easy to spill the water. Cupid dishes sold as soap dishes can also make interesting containers, see for example the arrangement on page 89.

ABOVE An ornate fan-shaped vase with a scalloped edge, with an arrangement of Spring flowers – *Osmanthus, Freesia, Fritillaria, Ranunculus, Helleborus foetidus, Myosotis, Scilla nutans, Muscari, Rosa, Narcissus, Hyacinthus, Eucalyptus, Allium, Pulsatilla.*

Baskets

There is a very large range of baskets which can be used for flowers today. They are usually made from rattan and cane and are imported from such places as the Far East, Portugal and Spain and come in many different shapes. Some baskets are made in England, but they are usually made in willow, which is more substantial than rattan and cane and appears heavier.

Most baskets have no lining so a container has to be found in which the flowers can be placed so as to appear as if they are arranged in the basket. Some people put the stems straight into one of the water-retaining foams wrapped in polythene to keep it moist and stop water dripping out. A glass pie dish is ideal for an oblong basket, and there are many bowls which will fit in a round basket.

Some baskets have metal linings and these are usually satisfactory but need painting to prevent them rusting; others may have a thin moulded plastic lining which eliminates rust but can be punctured easily when the netting is being fixed. Once the netting is fitted to the container it is best to leave it there and not to keep taking it in and out. This will also prevent the galvanizing on the netting from becoming cracked.

The large gilt Gainsborough basket, that tall high-handled shape that used to be so popular, is seldom seen today; it is expensive to buy and requires a lot of flowers to fill it. Another basket with a fairly high handle going from side to side, the big gilt oval-faced basket, is more likely to be seen filled with fruit at the back of a buffet table than filled with flowers but it is sometimes used for special occasions.

Baskets lend themselves to simple arrangements and look better in a cottage-type sitting room than in the grandeur of a large drawing room. Tiny square, oblong and round baskets are beautiful when arranged simply with mixed Spring or Summer flowers. They can also be filled with just one kind of flower.

LEFT ABOVE A collection of late-Summer garden flowers arranged in a Sussex trug. The flowers and foliages have been grouped together to avoid the spotty effect which often occurs in mixed groups. LEFT BELOW An oval cane hamper basket with its lid propped open, filled with Michaelmas daisies. BELOW Basket-type containers come in a variety of shapes, sizes and materials.

Wooden containers

Wood can be a sympathetic material for a container but it must have a waterproof lining.

The wooden trug—a speciality of the Sussex craftsman—is really a basket-type container (see page 34). A pie-dish is an ideal lining and can be bedded on moss or tissue paper to get it to fit firmly and level in the boat-shaped base of the basket. It looks particularly attractive filled with the more solid types of flowers, such as marigolds, wallflowers and sunflowers or, again, mixed collections of garden flowers.

Wooden boxes, such as those made in mahogany, make beautiful containers for flowers and are ideally suited to stand on a dresser or sideboard. Any interior fixtures will have to be taken out and a tin of suitable size (again, a baking tin is often ideal) used for a lining; sometimes the lid may be lined with velvet and this can be a feature; do not destroy it because the lid must be set up when the box is in use.

Wooden bowls, small half barrels, tubs and old wooden cheese presses make good cut-flower containers but are more likely to be filled with growing plants. This is perhaps due to the amount of cut flowers that are needed to fill them, and longer lasting plants would be cheaper to use in the long run.

Metal containers

Pewter
This is a useful colour for flowers, especially greys, mauves, purples and pinks. Many old pewter jugs, measures and mugs have pleasing lines and are easy to arrange. Flowers certainly last well in this type of container. A pewter plate is also a useful addition to a flower arranger's props—it will look good as a background and also be fun for a small arrangement. A pewter plate could also be used for a miniature garden, see page 116.

Silver
Silver is not often used nowadays compared with Victorian times, when trumpet vases and rose bowls were in most vase cupboards. A small silver basket or rose bowl remains perfect for a table setting but take care to line the vase first with brown paper, plastic or foil before placing wire netting into the container, and always clean the silver thoroughly after use. Silver demands certain types of flowers, as it can be so bright and shiny that it competes with the flowers. It takes soft delicate colours (mauves and pinks) and something rather sophisticated; on the other hand, some wild flowers, such as bluebells arranged with lacy foliage, can look very beautiful arranged in a silver sauce boat, for example.

RIGHT A variety of metal containers including a pewter jug, a silver rose bowl, a copper trough, a brass bowl with fluted edges and a copper jelly mould. RIGHT BELOW *Gentiana sino-ornata* with *Graphaleum* flower buds and *Cineraria* leaves arranged on a pewter plate with lumps of crystal which look like ice. BELOW The brightness of a silver container can make the flowers appear dull and must be used with care. Here an octagonal vase takes a mixed pink arrangement of *Astrantia, Alchemilla, Alstroemeria, Helleborus, Dianthus barbatus,* and *Sisyrinchium.*

Copper and brass

There are many good containers in these metals that were not designed to hold flowers yet are ideal for them, including such old kitchen equipment as saucepans, fish kettles and jelly moulds. The problem is to keep the containers clean and free from water marks which are difficult to clean off. Bad stains can be removed with salt and lemon or salt and vinegar: rub the surface really hard with a coarse cloth, rinse off and dry it thoroughly. Lacquering may be acceptable to some people to protect the metal but it detracts from the natural warm look, and the patina acquired over the years of cleaning with a soft cloth is lost. Once the lacquer starts to wear off, it will also be very difficult to get the container clean again.

Old copper has a pinkish tint to it and is much warmer-looking than brass; it lends itself to many of the soft apricot shades and Autumn tints. Brass is cooler and very attractive when used in conjunction with creams and lime greens. Both metals are excellent and the keen flower arranger is wise to collect as many shapes as possible.

Bronze

Few people have bronze vases today, but one very elegant shape is the 'Warwick cup' which is well-balanced and heavy.

A bronze vase calls for heavy looking flowers—you must, in fact, let the weight and importance of your flowers be reflected in the vase. You may safely fill it with heavy materials in proportion to its size.

Lead

At one time lead was favoured in the making of urns and window boxes for outside decoration but only a few of these remain. Lead is heavy but soft . and tends to split if not handled with care.

Wall vases

These can show flowers to really good advantage but great care must be taken to see that no syphoning of water occurs: the water level must be kept 1 cm ($\frac{1}{2}$ inch) below the rim of the vase and no leaf should hang over the rim at back or sides, otherwise the wallpaper may be marked. Fix the vase at the correct height and arrange the flowers with good downflowing lines.

LEFT The three-legged stand holding a glass dish, designed by Constance Spry for the Coronation. An arrangement of *Iris* leaves, *Delphinium, Clematis vitalba, Dianthus, Hydrangea, Scabious, Zinnia* 'Envy', *Nicotiana, Amaranthus caudatus* 'Viridis', *Aruncus, Eucalyptus.*

RIGHT The mirror trough, designed by Constance Spry. In the arrangement are *Erythronium, Hyacinthus orientalis, Phalaris arundinacea variegata, Helleborus orientalis, Hedera, Narcissus triandrus, Hebe, Polygonatum.*

LEFT Wall vases can be very useful, especially at parties. The flowers can be seen by everyone, yet kept well out of the way. In this arrangement are *Chaenomeles, Solidago, Hosta, Amaranthus caudatus* 'Viridis', *Helianthus, Nicotiana, Alchemilla, Chrysanthemum, Phalaris.*

Plastic and fibreglass

Although many people hate plastic, especially with flowers, little posy dishes and a few vases are quite useful and fairly cheap. The lightness of plastic may be a problem with some of the upright cherub type vases if they are not properly balanced. It may prove helpful to drill a hole in the back of the vase, fairly high up, and fill it with fine sand.

If you use plastic containers, keep to the white, black or green/white matt finishes, and look for a simple, pleasing shape. Very bright and shiny colours are rarely attractive for flowers in everyday use, although there are instances where brightly coloured plastic could be suitable. For example, the table for a children's party would look very gay with red, orange or yellow beakers and a centrepiece of Iceland or Californian poppies, arranged in a matching beaker or bowl, all on a brown hessian tablecloth.

Fibreglass is very strong yet light to handle and makes very good vases, especially the lead imitation which really does look natural. Again, being light, such a vase may fall over when full of tall foliage, etc., and it is a good idea to fill the base of the moulding with sand or gravel. Fibreglass pedestals are also useful and they can be painted any colour to suit the décor and should be filled with sand for safety.

Improvised vases

For the Coronation Mrs. Spry used two clever ideas; they were simple but adequate, and not too costly because we were still getting over the aftermath of World War II.

The first vase had to be suitable to stand on a round table seating about ten people. It was constructed of thin twisted wrought iron which was made into a three-legged stand and in this rested a glass dish. For a special effect the wrought iron was lightly touched with gold and a gold crown was fixed around the glass dish. The crown was made from buckram coated with gold paint, and on it were glued costume jewellery and a band of red velvet and mock ermine (white cellulose wool with black spots painted on it). These vases held the red flowers (including roses, carnations, azaleas) which were sent from San Remo. The vases stood on a tablecloth of pale blue silk and around the base of each vase was a garland of gold leaves and roses, made of artificial material. The cloth was finished with the E II R motif at four points.

The other vase, used for much larger arrangements on the buffet tables around the room, was designed on the same principle but, instead of glass dishes, large antique silver meat dish covers were used. The covers were turned upside down and were held in wrought iron stands.

Mechanics

PAGES 40–1 A
selection of
mechanics used in
flower arranging,
including a
pinholder, wire
netting, pebbles,
plastic foam.
BELOW Methods of
securing the netting:
tying it like a parcel
(left) and clipping
the ends of the wire
into the basketwork
(right). An end of
netting fixed round
an awkward stem
provides useful
support.

The mechanics are the means by which flowers can be positioned exactly as required within the container. They are essential to flower arranging as they are the foundation of the whole structure. So often one hears people say, 'I know what I want, but I can never get the flowers to stay in the correct place'. Once you understand the mechanics, however, you will find that you can work easily and with real pleasure.

Flower arranging has progressed a good deal since the days when flowers were stood in vases which had been stuffed with stems of evergreen to make the flowers all stand up straight, although this method is still used by some growers when showing their best garden blooms at the local flower show.

The mechanics should allow everything in the arrangement to have room and show to good advantage, the stems flowing gracefully from the centre of the vase and not standing at awkward angles, but the mechanics themselves must never show, whether they are wire netting, Oasis or any other aid.

Wire netting

Ordinary wire netting is the most generally useful of all the flower supporters. It should be fairly pliable and of a large mesh, 5 cm (2 inch) 0·71 mm (22 gauge) is the best because this will hold firmly yet bends easily in the hand. Never use the small-mesh netting because it is too rigid and when folded up will allow only the very thinnest stem entry into the vase.

Keep the netting clean and dry when not in use and it will last a long time. Always keep the same piece for each vase so you will not need to keep bending it to change the shape. Folding and bending cracks the galvanizing, causing the wire to rust and deteriorate rapidly. The amount of netting needed will depend on the shape and size of the vase but one should always aim to get four or five layers of netting in an upright vase, with the first layer just resting on the bottom. In a shallow dish three to four layers will be enough, especially in combination

ABOVE Securing the netting on vases with outcurving (left) and incurving (right) rims.
TOP Testing the firmness of the netting with bamboo canes.

with a pinholder. Too large a piece will make it difficult to fit in all the stems, while too small a piece will move about in the container and inevitably the stems will move around too. The amount used will also depend on personal preference. I always like to fix my own so that it is just right for me. After a while you will know exactly how you like the netting, and then you are well on the way to a good arrangement.

To check the firmness of netting before arranging the flowers, it is a good idea to thread a few small pieces of bamboo canes through the mesh to see how well the layers of netting are placed in the container. Always place the cut ends of the netting in the top of the vase because they can be clipped round the vase handle or rim for extra security. Also, an awkward stem which moves round could have one of these cut ends carefully twisted round it. This is not wiring the stem but just giving it a little extra hold and cannot be detected once the arrangement is completed.

There are various ways of fixing or holding wire netting firmly in place. Treating the whole container as though it were a parcel and tying the netting into position is the most elementary approach. This method is all right when using a shallow container, such as a large baking tin that is going to be placed where the container will be completely hidden. With such an arrangement it is a means of playing extra safe, and the telltale string can be hidden by materials coming well over the front; the string at the back of the vase can be secured to the window ledge for extra support and this will prevent the vase tipping over, as can so easily happen on a narrow ledge.

If string is used on a shallow container the flowers will almost certainly hide it when they are arranged. If the flowers are firm and well balanced the string can be cut away and they should stay in perfect position, but few people have the courage to do this!

A good idea is to use rubber bands—these can be bought in various colours and will seldom be seen if the arrangement is done well. They can be used for a jug, going round the top of the handle then over to the lip of the jug, and will be well hidden. Silver wire or fuse wire can also be used for tying the netting but it is rather more expensive.

If the container has an incurving rim you can place the netting under this then lift the central area up and it should remain firmly in place. On the other hand, if there is a rim to the outside of the vase, ears of netting can be pulled outwards and clipped over the rim, which will give a perfect hold.

It can be a problem to hide the mechanics in a glass goblet. Make a tangle of netting to fill the upper third of the vase, hooking the cut ends over the rim of the glass, and hide this with down-curving foliage, so that all the untidy netting and many of the stems are concealed.

If you use a valuable china vase or silver container, it is important to line it with thick brown paper or tin foil before attempting to place any wire netting in it. This will prevent scratching caused by sharp wire. Plastic-coated netting is easily available, although it is awkward to use as it is so thickly covered that it tends to move about in the vase and can only be firmly secured if it is tied with string. On the other hand, plastic-coated netting does last well because it does not rust.

In certain instances, wire netting can be successfully combined with a pinholder for extra weight. Similarly, it can be used in conjunction with plastic foam to soften the flow of the materials.

Pinholders

These are now available in many shapes and sizes and have become very popular. They are valuable for shallow containers and for flowers with thick stems where the elegance of the stems is of importance to the design of the arrangement.

Pinholders originated in Japan and consist of a heavy lead and alloy base into which sharp brass or steel pin-points have been set. As the pin-points may be of different lengths and distances apart, the right pinholder should be carefully chosen for the arrangement. It is a false economy to buy cheap pinholders because they will not last and are more expensive in the long run.

I seldom use a pinholder on its own—I prefer to use it in conjunction with a little wire netting so that support can be given to any thin-stemmed flowers which may be in the arrangement.

It is a tradition in England that the pinholder is always hidden, although this is not so in Japan. A little wire netting added to the vase eliminates the need to use any form of adhesive on the base of the pinholder, which is messy and unnecessary. When using pinholders, containers must be deep enough to hold at least 3·5 cm (1½ inches) of water if cut materials are to last for a reasonable length of time.

Keep pinholders dry when not in use, and do not force very thick woody material onto the pins without first splitting the material. You will only damage or bend the pins and weaken the holding capacity of the pinholder. The Oasis pinholder is another useful piece of equipment, and is particularly good for dried arrangements because it acts as a good balance for what can be a rather unstable arrangement in the weightless dry plastic foam.

Glass dome

For very heavy arrangements, the old-fashioned glass dome is worth considering. This does not normally suit home flower arrangements because flowers placed in ready-made holes have to stand in an upright position and it gives everything a 'surprised' look. The dome gives considerable weight to the vase, however, and if used in conjunction with netting for heavy materials such as stems of flowering cherry, this extra weight would be a great help. One or two of the upright stems can go through the netting into the glass dome, others can be threaded at the required angles through the netting and rest on top of the dome. A heavy pinholder could be used in just the same way though, and is far more versatile.

FAR LEFT ABOVE A special container with a well to hold the pinholder.
FAR LEFT BELOW A pinholder is useful for showing off these decorative stems (*Eucomis*) as it holds the stems firmly at the base. In English flower arranging the mechanics should never show, and some cover-up foliage would be necessary to complete this arrangement.
LEFT, ABOVE AND BELOW Materials arranged in a glass dome are bound to stand in an upright position which restricts the amount of stems that can be used and produces the 'surprised' look (top). When arranged in wire netting, however, the materials make a flowing arrangement, radiating from a centre point and having one or two materials to 'break' the rim of the vase (bottom). In the arrangements are *Chrysanthemum, Dianthus, Alstroemeria, Fagus*.

Sand and moss

Sand can be used to set little posies of flowers in small containers and is most effective when used on a flat round dish in which flower heads and petals have been set—a very formal type of arrangement, rather on the lines of a Victorian posy, which suits a low coffee table. Sand is heavy and inclined to scratch the surface of good china, so it should be used with care.

Moss is excellent for covering areas of soil in a planted dish or hiding an expanse of wire netting when arranging the first early Spring flowers in a copper pan or basket. It will give adequate support to a small group of flowers for a short period and, if kept moist, will maintain them without water. It is important to see that it is clean and free from any insect life before bringing it into the house. Always soak moss overnight in water before use.

ABOVE A collection
of useful mechanics.
Back row, left to
right: Florapak,
both the green cone
and the white
sphere which is
resting on a block of
Oasis are Styrofoam.
Middle row, left to
right: wire dome,
oblong pinholder,
flower tubes, the
Mazie and an Oasis
holder. Along the
front are cones
attached to square
sticks which sit
firmly in wire
netting.

Plastic foam: Oasis, Mosy and Florapak

Water-retaining modern aids to flower
arranging can be useful and certainly very
many people like using them. For beginners,
who do not seem to be happy with wire
netting, plastic foam is good because stems
will stay where they are placed and con-
sequently give confidence to the arranger,
but natural flowing lines are harder to
achieve and the finished arrangement often
has a rather stuffed look. Plastic foam en-
courages the use of straight stems placed at
all angles to give very drooping sides and an
exaggerated flow instead of curved-stemmed
materials which would flow naturally over
the edge of the vase rim. I would rather not
use these aids except in a very small container with little room for netting. While
they are essential for the florist whose
arrangements have to be transported, I consider them an unnecessary extra expense
for home use. Since flowers are often expensive, it seems better to forgo such extras and
spend the money on the actual flowers.

Oasis and Mosy are plastic foam in block

form or round units for posy bowls. They
are generally used wet and this can be easily
done by soaking them in a bucket for a few
hours. They must then be kept wet. It is no
use allowing them to dry then soaking them
again. If the blocks are turned over and used
from a different side, they can be used a few
times but once they fall to pieces they should
be discarded or completely broken up and
used like Florapak, to hold stems in a
container.

Some flowers are difficult to push into
Oasis and little holes must first be made with
a pencil so that when the stems are pressed
into it they do not snap off. I also find that
some flowers—anemones, for example—do
not last well in it.

For use with dried materials, Oasis and
Mosy should be used in their dry form.

Florapak has to be completely broken up
and soaked in a bath of water until it becomes
saturated. It is then packed into a bowl or
container and covered with a little wire
netting. The advantage of Florapak is that
it is good for soft stems which will not pene-
trate Oasis, and it can be used a few times
until it begins to smell. It is available in
white and green.

ABOVE Two blooms of *Paeonia* 'Sarah Bernhardt' are held in a thick glass goblet with polished stones which are both decorative and functional.

time when working with artificial materials, but it should not be sprayed with aerosol paint sprays as these will dissolve it.

Flower tubes

To introduce a fresh flower stem to a bowl of growing plants, flower tubes can be used. They are often found attached to the stems of orchids which have come in from abroad. They are usually made from a plastic tube or phial with a rubber top. The stem is pushed straight through the rubber top into the water and the whole tube can then be set among the plants.

Flower cones

Made of metal or plastic, flower cones can be fixed to pieces of firm cane or, better still, square sticks which bite into the netting and remain firm in the container. They can be disguised with neutral green paint.

They hold flowers high in a very large group when their natural stems could not reach into the vase, and are used for special occasions such as weddings and large receptions.

Build up a framework of cones in the vase and arrange them in front of the background foliage, then group the flowers in the cones to make the overall arrangement look as natural as possible. A small tangle of netting may be useful in the cones, and they should be kept filled with water if the flowers are to last. It may be necessary to top them up twice a day if the room is very warm.

I am very much against the modern idea of building up great frameworks of cones and Oasis to get a large group from short-stemmed flowers. This is a nightmare to maintain afterwards and it is impossible to really get the same effect as that achieved with natural long-stemmed materials.

The Mazie

This is the brand name of a commercially produced flower holder which is an oval mass of small-mesh wire netting fitted with one or more suction cups. Some people find it useful for light arrangements of very thin-stemmed flowers, but it is not at all suitable for heavy groups of thick-stemmed flowers and branches, and ordinary wire netting secured in place will do the same job more cheaply.

Styrofoam

A hard cellulose material available in various shapes, styrofoam does not take up water and is used solely to hold mounted dry materials in place. It is useful at Christmas

Decorative stones

Pebbles, shells and marbles, lumps of polished crystal and even coal can all be used most effectively, not only to hold stems in glass containers, but also to camouflage ungraceful stalks, to conceal the pinholder and wire netting, or to form part of a garden on a dish.

Indeed, by choosing such accessories in colours which blend with your main colour scheme, and by using them with imagination in your container, you can greatly add to the beauty of your design. For example, try using small pieces of bright coal with aubergines, purple spray carnations, grapes and slate green-grey *Begonia rex* leaves on a pewter dish. See page 37 for an example of lumps of crystal used on a pewter dish.

The principles
of arrangement

PAGES 48–9 A well balanced arrangement picking up the colourings in the room. Note in particular the way the roses give 'weight' to the centre of the arrangement, and the materials radiate from a centre point with good down-flowing lines and 'break' (conceal) the rim of the vase. The materials in this white urn-shaped vase are *Rosa* 'New Dawn' and *R.* 'Virgo', *Digitalis*, *Achillea mollis*, *Escallonia longleyensis* and *Hosta glauca*.

General hints

Rules and regulations have no place in flower arranging and what will appeal to one person may well not please another, but there are a few helpful guidelines. Over-arranged flowers are not restful to the eye and the final arrangement should not be a true geometric shape; let simplicity and a natural look be your guide. You are creating a picture with your fresh flowers, container and background, just as an artist does with a canvas, paints and paint brush.

I always prefer to visualize the finished arrangement and build it up as I go along, rather than keep placing pieces of foliage and flowers together to create an arrangement. In fact, I first decide where a vase of flowers can stand, then I choose the container and work out the colours which would be suitable. From this point, with the arrangement in mind, I pick and collect the necessary materials, first the background material and sides, choosing pieces which are the correct shape and which curve in the right direction. Next I select something for the front of the vase, then the filling-in materials. In working this way, one tends not to over-pick—so many arrangements are spoilt from overcrowding, because once a material has been picked or bought it seems such a waste not to use it. I always think back to one of Constance Spry's favourite sayings: 'If in doubt, leave it out!'

⚓ Always use flowers in their various stages of development—buds, half-open flowers, and open flowers.

⚓ Flowers will need to be of different lengths—no two flowers of the same length should be next to each other. Have an 'in and out' effect rather than a flat level appearance.

⚓ Group the flowers into different shapes and colours and bring these through the arrangement in sweeps rather than in blocks of single colours.

⚓ Set the vase in the correct position before starting. If it has handles check that they are correctly positioned on either side when facing you. If it has a square base this should be absolutely square on when viewed from the front.

⚓ Try to arrange the flowers at the height at which they are to stand: by lowering or raising the vase you will get a different view of the flowers, so do the arrangement in the permanent position if you can.

⚓ Grade out the flowers into sizes, normally keeping the larger ones, especially the dark colours, to the centre. This does not necessarily apply once you have experience and a natural instinct for pleasing proportion and balance.

3

4

All stems should radiate from a centre point. Make use of curved stems, placing them in such a way that they flow from the container naturally. Flowers should not be mangled to conform to a geometric shape.

Always look at the flowers from the sides as well as at the front to see that they stand well in the vase.

Allow the flowers to flow over the rim of the vase, coming well out at the front.

Arrange the outline first and carefully prune out any unwanted pieces which make it appear too heavy. One or two stems should point slightly backwards to give the arrangement a less flat look and make all the difference to the vase.

Place the back stems about three quarters of the way across the vase for a facing arrangement. The area of wire netting at the back of these stems should be covered with a few short pieces of foliage to make it appear tidy and finished.

If you have only one or two flowers of a certain kind or colour, place them close together to give them more impact.

Avoid a 'surprised look' at all costs by always having a leaf or two to break the hard rim of the vase.

THIS PAGE Stages in the arrangement of a Summer basket.
1. *Polygonatum multiflorum, Paeonia* leaves and *Tellima grandiflora* set the height and width.
2. Three *Bergenia* leaves, radiating outwards, form the centre. *Camassia esculenta* and *Polygonum bistorta* are added.
3. Pink *Aquilegia* is added through the centre of the group and *Lonicera* is placed over the rim of the basket, to the left of the handle, to 'break' the hard rim of the container and link flowers and container together.
4. *Syringa vulgaris, S.* 'Preston' and *Paeonia* 'Madame Louis Henri' flowers are now added deep down, to give centre weight.
5. The finishing touches are made, making sure that the handle can be seen and, if necessary, be used to pick up the arrangement.

Colour

Formal theories of colour matching are based upon the position in the spectrum of the seven colours in the rainbow (red, orange, yellow, green, blue, indigo and violet), and colour theorists argue that certain combinations of colours are preferable to others. This may be so for certain purposes but in flower arrangement I have always found it advisable to discard any such preconceptions about colours.

Some people will go for bright, clear colours, others will favour the more subtle shades. Colour is an intensely personal affair about which it would be unwise to be dogmatic. Younger people often like bright colourings—for example, orange and blue together which is perfectly correct according to the colour wheel although I would rarely think of putting these two together. These rather hard colour combinations are often only fashionable for a short time and people soon tire of them, whereas one can live with the softer tones and shades for much longer.

On the other hand, to let personal prejudice prevent you from experimenting with possible colours is very limiting. We do not know whether everyone sees the same colours and I have often heard two people give different names to what seems to me to be the same colour. Try all colours in different combinations and see for yourself what effect they have. Different lights and backgrounds will change the colour effects. Keep an open mind and do not be ruled by the colour wheel. You may hit upon unexpectedly satisfactory results during your experiments. We have all heard such comments at a show as 'I should never have dared to put those two colours together but don't they look nice?'

Although we do not have rules about colour in flower arranging, some formal knowledge may be required, especially if you are going to enter the competition field.

Complementary colours are situated opposite each other on the colour wheel, such as yellow and violet, orange and blue, and red and green.

Analogous colours are situated next to each other. They are related, the primary colour dominating the other colour.

A **shade** is a colour with the addition of black.

A **tint** is a colour with the addition of white.

A **monochromatic** colour scheme is made up of tints and shades of one colour. It often causes some difficulty because a general colour such as pink can be dominated by blue pinks (such as the 'Carol' rose) or orange pinks (such as 'Doris' border carnations) and these do not really go together.

Greens are much loved by some, others find them dull and uninteresting and wish for a little colour to be added. The use of mixed greens relies largely on contrast of form, with different shapes next to each other—round leaves, sword-shaped leaves, fern fronds, ivy trails and so on. When assembling the material one looks for as wide a range of tones and shades as possible; pale, dark, grey-green, blue-green, yellow-green and variegated leaves. Constance Spry was particularly fond of mixed greens and introduced many interesting plants into arrangements which had never been used before. It was she who first used mixed greens for wedding bouquets.

Green groups have the advantage of lasting a long time and can easily be kept looking nice by replacing the odd leaf that dies. Green is a restful colour and suits most rooms. It is valuable in Summer as a contrast to the more brilliant Summer flowers in the garden. It has a toning-down effect when used with coloured flowers so should not be used for a really brilliant group.

Yellow tends to light up a mixed group of flowers and is particularly valuable during the long Winter months when there is little colour about. There is a wide range of yellows and the citron (greeny) yellow is a very popular colour with greens and mixed pastel shades.

Yellow and blue go well together: yellow and pink are not considered to do so, yet the beautiful rose 'Peace' is yellow, flushed with pink on the edges of its petals. I believe it is the way that colours are used that is of importance. Try to blend the yellow-cream and lime-green foliages such as hosta and elaeagnus with yellow flowers, so that the foliage complements the flower colour.

BELOW LEFT The colour wheel.
BELOW RIGHT This is a true clashing red arrangement. It stands in a copper bowl and contains a wide range of red colourings. The materials are *Rhus cotinus* 'Foliis purpureis', *Rosa rubrifolia, Prunus, Gladiolus, Atriplex hortensis rubra, Zinnia, Dahlia, Kentranthus, Geranium, Antirrhinum, Scabiosa, Amaranthus caudatus.*

Orange is a hard colour but, when mixed with browns, yellows and greens, can give very warm and striking effects. It is, perhaps, rather 'hot' for summer arrangements but lovely in the autumn, especially when arranged in copper and brass containers. Again, use foliages to bring out the colour.

Red is the colour for really magnificent effects and calls for courage when it is used. The wider the range of reds used, the better the result. It is fatal to weaken halfway—work through crimson, rose, ruby, vermilion, magenta, even orange. No single colour should stand out but the whole should light up with an exciting glowing note of red. Most, if not all, the green foliage should be cut out and red foliages such as prunus and beetroot, added instead.

Blue, although a lovely colour, can be difficult to use. It is not good under artificial light and may well be lost at night if used as a decoration for a dinner party. It can be absorbed by a background of grey stone walling and a large group used in a church can appear to have gaps in it from a distance if the blue flowers do not show up, so in such a position it needs a good background foliage. Blue colourings are cool in the daytime and look well in a mixed garden basket as a Summer decoration.

Pastel colours—soft pinks, blues, mauves, lavenders and creamy yellows—are always a delight when mixed with citron-green and grey foliages. They look well in most positions and seldom fail to please. They are perfect in soft grey china, grey-green coloured pewter and silver containers.

Mixed colours, when cleverly used can be lovely and one has only to study some of the Dutch masters' paintings to see this. It is always fun to try and make a Dutch group from a few stems of interesting materials. The best time for this is late Spring, or groups of mixed garden flowers in Summer.

Room decoration

The use of flowers is an important aspect of interior decoration and the flower arrangements should form an integral part of the room. Some people contend that well-arranged groups of flowers, being beautiful in themselves, cannot look wrong, but the flowers should fit happily into their surroundings and not be too prominent.

It is of great importance to see a room first before deciding what to use in it. The colouring of the materials should relate to one of the main furnishing colours within that room. One room may call for reds while another may be so busy and colourful that just green and white is all that is required. Certain dye colours are not found in any growing material, so if the furnishing colours are difficult in this respect concentrate on complementing just one or two shades with flowers.

The position of flowers in the room is of the utmost importance and the best effect is generally achieved by concentrating on one or two large groups rather than having lots of little arrangements dotted about here and there as was done in Victorian times. On the other hand, I have seen a small cottage sitting room which had a few shelves on a wall and on these were many small arrangements of the most glorious flowers which looked as if they were pieces of china. It was quite beautifully done and very effective.

The personality of the room should control the flower decoration. The most important factor is the 'quality' of the room or some dominant feature, that is, its immediate impression, whether it is austere, dignified, simple, elaborate, pretty or 'modern'. A modern room, for example, may call for a simple line arrangement whereas the rather old-fashioned type of décor can take many more flowers in the arrangement. There will usually be some special feature in any room around which you may build your flower scheme; this may be a beautiful mirror or picture, an alcove, the wall colourings, or the colouring of the curtains or carpet.

Groups of flowers in a room usually look best when set against the solid background of a wall or a curtain with the light shining on them. They are most satisfactorily lighted from above by a spotlight or, if standing in an alcove, they can be lighted from above and behind with a warm light.

One of the most difficult tasks for the flower arranger is to plan flowers for a highly decorated room containing a lot of furniture. It may be necessary to provide a specially restful background. If you are working against a very strongly patterned wallpaper, a plain wall hanging could be positioned

BELOW These flowers and their container were chosen to match the dominant colourings in the room. The chrysanthemums are single stems of flowers and buds taken from three compound stems of florist's *Chrysanthemum* 'White Marble'. Other materials are *Hyacinthus, Scilla nutans* and *Eucalyptus*.

behind the flowers. This should harmonize with the wall colouring and can be in linen, shantung, hessian or a woven grass-cloth. Choose the right type of flowers for the background. Such specially contrived backgrounds are useful in difficult circumstances but they should be used with discretion because flowers always look best when they fit naturally with the rest of the room. Rich colours often look well in a book-lined room; they seem to associate well with the bindings, and elaborate vases can be used here to good effect.

Flowers should never be lit from below or stood on a glass base with a light in it: all this will do is to illuminate the mass of stems if using a glass container and also warm the flower water which may encourage breeding bacteria and create an unpleasant smell.

Certain flowers with translucent petals take on added glow and beauty when placed against the light. Iceland and Shirley poppies are a good example; they look particularly beautiful arranged against a window with the sun coming through them.

If flowers are being used to emphasize a particular decorative object in the room they should be placed near it; for instance, red flowers, designed to pick up the tones of a red picture, could be arranged below it in a low horizontal way; or the group could be slender and pointed in shape and set at one side of the picture. In either case take care that the flowers or leaves do not obscure any part of the picture.

For smaller arrangements, various objects may be placed close by the flowers to complement them, such as a pewter platter, a polished copper tray, a piece of silver or a decorative china figure.

Flowers for a party are best placed on a mantelpiece where they are up out of the way and can be seen by all. Flowers on low tables on such an occasion are quite lost after the first few people have arrived. If the flowers are in front of a mirror, remember to tidy the back! Also, use fewer stems in the vase because mirrors tend to multiply the flowers.

Table flowers should be considered carefully. They should be simpler for a lunch than for an evening meal, both in their content and arrangement. For a special dinner, a candlestick may be suitable as the flowers would be lifted well off the table. Arrangements in candlesticks should be small, light and flowing and not have large flowers around the base of the candle as is so often seen. It is generally considered correct that table flowers should be low to allow a clear view across the table but this is not an infallible rule.

ABOVE The flowers arranged in this china urn pick up the colours of the painted flowers on it. They are *Malus floribunda, Primula vulgaris* and *P. denticulata, Alyssum saxatile, Muscari botrioides, Euonymus radicans variegatus*. The decorative copper kettle complements and enhances the arrangement.

Spring

Spring is really the beginning of the flower arranger's year. By **March** gardens should be showing signs of change after the cold Winter. The extra daylight hours and higher temperatures encourage the buds to burst, only to be set back again by the occasional cold winds and frosts. Many of the Winter flowers and foliages will still be useful.

USEFUL MATERIALS
Azalea, Camellia, Cyclamen coum, Daphne mezereum, Echeveria retusa hybrida (from florist), *Iris tuberosa* syn. *Hermodactylus tuberosus, Lachenalia* (from florist), *Larix, Magnolia stellata, Muscari, Narcissi,* *Primula polyanthus, Primula vulgaris, Prunus, Ribes sanguineum, Viburnum.*

Perhaps the best time of year for the flower arranger is **April**. It is then that there are so many interesting things available in the flower shops, gardens and the hedgerow.

USEFUL MATERIALS
Azalea, Betula, Camellia, Cineraria (from florist), *Erythronium dens-canis, Euphorbia, Fritillaria imperialis, Hosta, Hyacinthus, Lathyrus* (forced, from florist), *Magnolia soulangeana, Osmanthus delavayi, Primula, Rhododendron.*

May is often a good month for weather and a very big change takes place around the countryside. The majority of the trees are fully covered with fresh leaves and many are also in full flower during this month so this is a good time for big arrangements with large arching sprays of blossom.

USEFUL MATERIALS
Antirrhinum (from florist), *Arisarum, Centaurea, Convallaria majalis, Cytisus, Datura, Doronicum, Euphorbia, Fritillaria meleagris, Gentiana acaulis, Hydrangea* (from florist), *Matthiola, Myosotis, Polygonatum, Primula auricula, Ranunculus* (from florist), *Sorbus aria, Syringa, Trollius, Tulipa, Viburnum opulus sterile.*

PAGES 56–7
White forms of narcissi together with cowslips are simply arranged with foliages cut from the garden. The flowers are brought through the arrangement in groups for a more striking effect.

The white footed bowl is standing on a polished table and it is the reflection on the table and the way the light shows through the petals of the narcissi which emphasises the delicacy of the arrangement.

The use of flowers at all stages of their development is very important in flower arranging; note in particular the angular bud on the left hand side.

LEFT
The container for this arrangement is an old brass ink stand, in which a small glass bowl is placed to hold the wire netting, flowers and water.

Garden foliages provide the framework for the arrangement. A few cream cineraria have been used and they are the last of the flower heads from a plant whose foliage is no longer decorative at this time of year. The hyacinth stems are the secondary spikes from a pot of growing bulbs used for decoration just after Christmas. They looked untidy on the old bulbs, but cut and arranged here they have a new lease of life.

BELOW
This is a collection of short-stemmed Spring bits rather than an arrangement of any set pattern or shape. They have been placed in a shallow round bowl, making a useful table centre for a small dinner party. When only very little room is available the use of a small posy such as this is often very successful.

PAGES 56–7
Daphne pontica
Primula veris
Narcissus including
    'Actaea' and
    'Camellia'
Cymbidium
Callistemon

LEFT
Forsythia ovata
Philadelphus
Euonymus
Freesia
Ranunculus
Hyacinthus
Cineraria
Helleborus foetidus
Fritillaria meleagris

BELOW
Muscari latifolium
Hyacinthus
Primula vulgaris
Scilla
Dianthus
Narcissus

This shallow shell-edged oval vase makes an effective centre for a rectangular table. The container is so shallow that in addition to being fitted with wire netting, a small pin-holder has been fixed in the centre.

The soft silver-grey lamb's tongues have been used before any flowers have formed and this gives them extra stem length. Care must be taken to see that the thick felty leaves are always held above the water level as they readily syphon water from the vase.

The sharp lime-green flower heads of euphorbia have been brought up through the arrangement from side to side.

The arrangement is completed with pale-coloured cultivated bluebells. Cultivated bluebells have rather stiff thick fleshy stems and wild ones would probably have created a softer effect; they would certainly have been a deeper shade.

RIGHT

This pleasing arrangement stands in a shallow grey fluted fruit bowl. Wide varie-gated aspidistra and large artichoke leaves at the base give way to narrow spiky foliage at the top. All the stems flow from a centre point and this is emphasized by the deep purple grapes giving extra weight at the centre. The English iris have been chosen for their colour which complements the grapes.

The flowers are held in position by wire netting and a pinholder, and the stem of the grapes has been hooked into the wire at the rim of the vase.

BELOW RIGHT

Two bunches of mixed wallflowers are ar-ranged in a hamper basket. The lid has been propped up with a short length of cane and contributes to the cottage-style effect of the arrangement. Wallflowers look well in simple containers. They are usually more effective when arranged on their own and here the stems have all been cut to different lengths for variety rather than a flat mass of flowers. Stems should be hammered and all foliage below the water line must be removed as the wallflower is a member of the cabbage family and the water will quickly start to smell.

Wallflowers are not long lasting but they offer a wealth of colour and a lovely scent.

RIGHT
Cynara scolymus
Tulipa
Rhododendron
Erica
Lamium
Iris xiphioides
Ixia
Senecio greyii
Hedera
Pelargonium
*Aspidistra elatior
 variegata*
Helleborus orientalis
Eucalyptus gunnii

BELOW
Scilla nutans
Stachys lanata
Euphorbia cyparisias

BELOW RIGHT
Cheiranthus

Step-by-step arrangement

1. Whitebeam is an excellent background foliage because it has such well-shaped branches. Here its silvery green foliage looks well against the pale green background. It needs a good firm anchorage as the branches are heavy and for this arrangement a wide bowl has been used, containing a heavy pin-holder and a mass of wire netting raised well above the vase rim for extra support.

The stems all radiate from a centre point and flow well over the vase rim. Provided the vase is kept full, stems positioned horizontally have access to as much water as those standing upright.

2. Six stems of double cherry are added next and they too flow from a centre point and look comfortable.

3. Seven stems of euphorbia and a few artichoke leaves complete the arrangement, giving weight to the centre of the vase.

The container is no longer visible and only serves the purpose of holding water and anchoring the stems.

Sorbus aria lutescens
Prunus serrulata
 'Kansan'
Euphorbia characias
Cynara scolymus

3

LEFT
Small arrangements of mixed green foliages can be made at any time of the year. All the foliages and seed heads for this arrangement came from my small city garden except for a few cuttings from houseplants.

The vase is made from a real shell fixed to a dolphin base. It is quite small (compare its size with the paperbacks on the shelf above) so the stems are held in a little block of Oasis to allow them to flow at angles from the shell yet still receive moisture.

ABOVE
So often in Spring yellow flowers are from the narcissus family, but here is a pint-sized pewter tankard containing small yellow roses and spray carnations which are yellow flecked with pink. These florist's flowers are the sort of flowers one might receive as a gift purchased from a flower shop, and for the arrangement they have been supplemented with garden foliage. The carnations are used at various stages of development and the buds will open out in the arrangement.

LEFT
Geranium
Helleborus
Hedera
Zantedeschia
Osmanthus
Erica
Ruta graveolens
Passiflora caerulea
Veronica
Euonymus

ABOVE
Eucalyptus gunnii
Osmanthus delavayi
Rosa 'Spanish Sun'
Dianthus
Euphorbia robbiae

ABOVE

This sophisticated table centre for a dinner party is arranged in a silver candlestick fitted with an aluminium candle cup. The candle cup was originally designed in glass by Constance Spry to hold flowers at a dinner given by government ministers for Her Majesty The Queen.

The materials are arranged in wire netting and flow gracefully over the edge of the candle cup. The flower stems have been cut quite short and the flowers are grouped together rather than dotted about to make a greater impact.

RIGHT

This cheerful Springtime arrangement of daffodils and narcissi with mixed foliage gives a pleasing decoration for a cottage dining room.

Daffodils are difficult to arrange and need to face in all directions to look natural. Simple containers suit them and here a rectangular basket completes the rustic effect and complements the simple style of the dining room.

Viburnum foliage with small flower sprays has been used to fill in the base of the arrangement and hide the netting.

Not all bluebells are blue, and here pink, white and blue cultivated bluebells have been used in equal quantities. They were arranged in the vase first and then the bare stems were filled in with small pieces of euphorbia.

Euphorbia and bluebells are both extremely useful Spring garden materials and they go well together for simple arrangements.

The container for this arrangement is a round frosted-glass bowl, but as it is an all-round arrangement for a low wooden table the vase is hardly visible.

BELOW
Narcissus
Salix
Corylus
Viburnum tinus

RIGHT
Scilla nutans
Euphorbia robbiae

Summer

June immediately conjures up roses in the minds of flower arrangers. Many flowers and foliages are very prolific in this month and the decorator has a great choice.

USEFUL MATERIALS

Alchemilla, Astrantia, Centaurea cyanus, Delphinium, Dianthus, Digitalis, Eremurus, Escallonia, Geranium, Lilium, Lupinus, Nigella, Paeonia, Papaver, Passiflora caerulea, Philadelphus, Pyrethrum, Rosa, Spartium junceum, Tilia.

The months of **July** and **August** normally see a change in the overall flower colourings in the garden. Brighter colours creep in as many mixed annuals are now in flower. Towards the end of August one should start to select materials for drying and preserving for the Winter months ahead.

USEFUL MATERIALS

Achillea, Angelica, Chrysanthemum, Delphinium, Echinops, Eryngium, Lathyrus, Lilium, Nicotiana, Phlox, Rosa, Salvia, Scabiosa, Solidago, Veratum nigrum.

PAGES 68–9

A glorious collection of old-fashioned garden roses in the drawing room at Constance Spry's own home in Berkshire. The container is a Dresden china fruit dish, lined with a simple white china bowl.

ABOVE

A pretty pink Wedgwood powder bowl is the container for this delicate arrangement of short-stemmed flowers. Sweet peas and roses have a pleasing perfume, making this a delightful arrangement for a bedroom. The lid is propped up with a length of cane, and a small piece of Oasis holds the flowers.

RIGHT

This white double rose has a lovely scent and makes an attractive table setting when simply arranged with its own foliage. Great care is needed when using glass containers to ensure that the mechanics do not show and the water is clean.

PAGES 68–9

Rosa 'Charles de Mills'
    'Cardinal Richelieu'
    'Madame Ernst Calvat'
    'Madame Isaac Pereire'
    'Belle de Crécy'
    'Constance Spry'

ABOVE

Rosa 'Jenny Wren'
Lathyrus
Alchemilla

RIGHT

Rosa 'Alba Maxima'

LEFT
The rose named after Constance Spry has a lovely muddled centre and a delightful scent. It is very heavy when fully open and tends to hang over like an open paeony. Unfortunately it only flowers during June for a short period and there is no second crop in early Autumn.

The flowers are arranged to be viewed from above as they are standing on a low glass-topped coffee table.

RIGHT
Sweet peas are available in such an attractive range of colours that their success in an arrangement is often the result of a careful choice of colours. Here they have been chosen to complement the décor of the room which is predominantly blue.

Green alchemilla, dotted throughout the arrangement provide an interesting contrast to the sweet peas. Only a few alchemilla leaves are needed to break the rim of the vase at the front and soften the harsh angular look of the container. Care must always be taken when using silver containers as their bright shine can easily conflict with the delicacy of flowers.

BELOW RIGHT
The soft grey colour of this alabaster tazza tones well with the pink flowers and green-grey eucalyptus foliage. As the bowl is very shallow the flowers are arranged in a glass dish on a pinholder with a little wire netting.

Antirrhinums and the buds of Doris border carnations make the outline for this triangular-shaped arrangement. Euonymus runs through it from the left and the large well-marked arum leaf gives added weight to the centre.

LEFT
Even a small bunch of border carnations can make a successful room decoration. Here they are arranged in a half-pint pewter tankard. The stems are cut to different lengths to give variety and depth to the arrangement, and the flowers' own foliage, buds and shoots add interest.

ABOVE LEFT *Rosa* 'Constance Spry'	**RIGHT** *Antirrhinum* *Dianthus × allwoodii* 'Doris'
ABOVE RIGHT *Lathyrus* *Alchemilla mollis*	*Dianthus* 'Pink Jim' *Euonymus latifolius* *variegatus*
LEFT *Dianthus × allwoodii* 'Doris'	*Helleborus orientalis* *Arum italicum pictum* *Viburnum carlesii* *Eucalyptus gunnii* *Rosa* 'Carol'

ABOVE
Sorbus aria
Cynara scolymus
Digitalis
Lupinus
Allium
Matthiola
Syringa 'Preston'
Rhododendron ponticum
Rosa 'Magenta'

RIGHT
Escallonia 'Apple Blossom'

ABOVE
The corner of a room is often a good place in which to stand flowers as they show up well yet are out of the way. This arrangement has been made to suit the shape of the recessed wall and look comfortable in its surroundings without appearing contrived.

The pewter measure container not only suits the colour of the flowers, but its heavy nature helps it to take the 'height' of the materials in it. Substantial-looking flowers such as these would look quite unbalanced in a delicate container.

RIGHT
Just five shapely stems of escallonia in a narrow-necked coffee pot constitute this elegant arrangement. Choose thin-stemmed branches in preference to thick-stemmed pieces when using a narrow-necked vase as you will be able to fit in more pieces. Always remember to let the natural shape of the branch dictate its positioning – a straight piece forced to curve over the side of the container will never look happy. Compare this with the step-by-step arrangement of whitebeam branches on page 62.

BELOW

A tall mantelpiece is a good place on which to stand flowers, especially for a party, as they are well out of reach yet easily seen.

The container for this arrangement of mixed reds is a shallow mirror trough. Being long and low it is well suited to a mantelpiece position. Note the way in which the three compound heads of roses have been used in the centre, giving weight and depth of colour, while the single-headed stems of the sweet williams are on the outside. The foliage adds flowing lines to the arrangement.

BOTTOM

Old-fashioned roses look best when simply arranged with their own foliage (see also pages 71 and 72). Here just two varieties are used: the climbing 'La Follette' is the pink rose and 'Blanc Double de Coubert' is the white. This was the rose chosen by Constance Spry for a decoration in the retiring room for H.M. the Queen straight after her coronation when a simple basket was filled to overflowing with this sweet-smelling white rose. The flowers are used in various stages of development and will open out.

ABOVE RIGHT
Rosa 'Rosemary Rose'
Dianthus barbatus
Symphoricarpos

RIGHT
Rosa 'Blanc Double de
Coubert'
Rosa 'La Follette'

(see page 53)

ABOVE
This is not quite a clashing red arrangement (see page 53) as a few green rhododendron leaves have been used to break the rim of the vase, and the crab apple has some green colouring. Nevertheless it achieves a similarly stunning effect, enhanced by the rich shiny surface of the inlaid table.

ABOVE
Malus atrosanguinea
Syringa
Bergenia cordifolia
  purpurea
Rhododendron
Geranium cerise
Tulipa

ABOVE
As sweet peas have a rather fussy outline, a clear-cut foliage such as hosta complements them well. Compare this arrangement of sweet peas with that on page 73 where alchemilla was used giving a dotted effect to the arrangement.

RIGHT
The warm colour of this arrangement is unusual for Summer but it would be a good decoration for a cool evening. Note how the weight of colour from the orange lily is kept to the centre of the vase and the lighter colours flow in sweeps outwards from the centre. The yellow ivy foliage used at the base of this arrangement is a useful plant for the flower arranger to grow if a little wall space is available.

FAR RIGHT
This marble and alabaster vase lends itself to arrangements with flowing lines where each leaf and flower is placed in a very clear-cut position. The lines of the arrangement tie up with the lines of carving on the rim and stem of the vase. This is a good style of arrangement to show off materials of special interest. Here the five clematis are the focal point even though they are not centrally placed.

LEFT
Lathyrus
Hosta undulata

BELOW
Cordyline purpurea
Gladiolus
Allium siculum
Alchemilla mollis
Achillea 'Moonshine'
Lilium pyrenaicum
Lilium 'Enchantment'
Rosa 'Golden Rain'
Rosa 'Pitica'
Antirrhinum
Hedera
Lonicera
Kalanchoe
Anemone pulsatilla
Muscari
Euonymus japonicus
   albo-marginatus
Elaeagnus pungens
   'Aureo-Maculata'

ABOVE
Heuchera	*Geranium crispum*	*Echeveria retusa*	*Rosa chinensis viridis*
Clematis florida	*variegatum*	*Begonia cleopatra*	*Iris foetidissima*
'Bicolor'	*Geranium* 'Golden	*Sedum sieboldii variegata*	*Asparagus meyerii*
	Harry Hieover'	*Lunaria biennis*	*Ballota pseudodictamnus*

79

ABOVE
Lupinus
Nigella
Dianthus
Alchemilla mollis
Rosa 'La Minuet'
Campanula
Digitalis
Dianthus barbatus
Nepeta
Phlomis

LEFT
Tilia
Cynara
Lilium 'Regale'
Paeonia 'Sarah
   Bernhardt'

LEFT

Branches of stripped lime make a very attractive background foliage. Make sure that every leaf is stripped off the branches so the bracts show clearly and to good effect. The three artichoke leaves at the centre of the vase help to link the container and the flowers. The stripped lime and lilies, which have a tendency to look rather light and airy, would otherwise be out of keeping with the heavy vase.

The colour of the paeonies, dotted through the arrangement, picks up the pink of the lily buds.

ABOVE

A heavy white ceramic vase with a handle each side holds a collection of mid-Summer flowers picked from a herbaceous border, together with a few side shoots of stripped lime and three commercial roses.

The lupins which have been filled with water and plugged are now beginning to take up natural curves.

FAR RIGHT

This is an all round arrangement for a low coffee table. It stands in a shallow pewter fruit dish containing a dome of wire netting. The colourings, which include a whole range of pink and mauve tones, have been chosen to blend in with the predominant colouring of the furnishing fabric. Although many of these tones may be said to clash, the overall effect is a good blend. See also the clashing red arrangement on page 53. A few extra leaves at the centre make up for the lack of foliage on such stems as the annual scabious.

BELOW

A bold all-round arrangement of red and white roses, chosen to carry through the colour scheme of the room. The flowers are simply arranged with plenty of their own foliage in a white tazza.

BELOW RIGHT

Fruit always adds importance to a group of flowers and here is a splendid group of flowers and fruit arranged in a copper pan. This would be a very suitable decoration for a sideboard or buffet table at a party.

The netting has been kept high to support the fruit and a heavy pinholder has been placed at the centre-back of the container to weight the pineapple. The pineapple itself has a piece of cane pushed into it to give it the necessary height. The grapes have been kept in their bunches and bedded down on a few leaves to stop them getting tangled in the netting.

The flowers are arranged in the usual way, flowing from a centre point. The exotic torch lily, *Gloriosa*, is a climbing lily which is easy to grow in a greenhouse and very long lasting.

RIGHT

Hydrangea
Dahlia
Anemone
Spiraea douglassii
Scabious
Delphinium
Phlox
Senecio
Artemesia

BELOW

Rosa 'Paul's Scarlet'
Rosa 'Iceberg'

BELOW
Cordyline purpurea
Polygonatum multiflorum
Smilacina racemosa
Rhododendron 'Ghent'
Gloriosa rothschildiana
Iris pseudacorus
Lilium 'African Queen'
    and *L. pyrenaicum*
Gerbera
Euphorbia palustris and
    E. robbiae
Aralia
Allium siculum

Autumn

PAGES 84–5
The rich colours of Autumn make a glorious display. The container for this arrangement is a plastic plant saucer standing on a flat round basket and the stems are arranged in Oasis with just a single layer of wide-mesh netting over the top to help achieve a flowing arrangement. The flowering hops flow attractively over the edge of the shelf.

BELOW
A simple arrangement can quickly brighten up a narrow dark hallway. Here just five rudbeckia flowers and a little osmanthus foliage make a practical upright arrangement in a modern cylindrical pottery vase. The osmanthus softens the rather severe lines of the rudbeckia stems which have very little foliage of their own.

PAGES 84–5
Gladiolus
Dahlia
Helianthus
Azalea (foliage)
Symphoricarpos
Humulus
Begonia
Solidago
Kniphofia
Cactus
Nicotiana
Chrysanthemum

LEFT
Rudbeckia
Osmanthus

September is the month of dahlias and the Michaelmas daisy. Dahlias are heavy flowers so arrangements are often fairly large.

USEFUL MATERIALS
Agapanthus, Amaranthus, Aster, Brassica, Chrysanthemum, Clematis vitalba, Cobaea, Crinum, Dahlia, Eucomis, Euonymus europaeus, Freesia (from florist), *Gentiana sino-ornata, Gladiolus* (from florist), *Humulus, Phlox, Phytolacca, Reseda, Rosa, Veratum nigrum, Verbena, Vitis, Zinnia.*

The Autumnal colourings are enhanced by the appearance of fruit and berries in **October**. The intensity of the Autumnal tint varies annually, being far more colourful in a dry Autumn.

USEFUL MATERIALS
Achillea, Aster, Chrysanthemum, Colchicum, Dahlia, Delphinium, Hydrangea, Nerine, Rosa, Rudbeckia, Zinnia.

ABOVE
Often a few leftover pieces from larger arrangements can make an ideal group for a small occasional table. Here, for example, the fine-leaved eucalyptus stems are the basal side shoots removed from larger stems, and there are short stems of calendula and chrysanthemum. The use of some chrysanthemum buds helps to keep the arrangement from looking too heavy. The berries are from privet in its early green stage: when black, two or three months later, they are very useful in Winter groups.

The pure white Autumn crocus is less common than the purple variety but it is delightful when arranged with just a few other flowers. The pompom dahlias are off-white with pink backs to their petals, picking up the colour of the freesia buds. The open freesia links up with the two annual scabious, and a bunch of elderberries gives weight to the centre of the group. Variegated ivy is the backing foliage.

RIGHT
This attractive arrangement makes use of a range of pink tones, offset by a little green, for its effect. The snapdragons and grass heads make the height of the arrangement while the snowberries, tinged with pink, break the rim of the vase. The two semi old-fashioned roses and a hydrangea head give weight to the centre.

ABOVE	RIGHT
Colchicum	*Antirrhinum*
Hedera	*Symphoricarpos*
Dahlia 'Pompom'	*Rosa* 'Dream Girl'
Scabious	*Hydrangea*
Sedum	*Pennisetum*
Lathyrus	
Freesia	
Sambucus	
Polygonum	

LEFT
A formal urn-shaped vase generally calls for an arrangement with clean-cut materials, but here the setting, dominated by the colourings of the paintings, suits this group even though the flowers have a rather fussy outline. The white chrysanthemum is a delicate American spray which is very useful because it breaks down well into many side shoots for easy arranging. The seakale is wild, collected from the seashore.

BELOW
A wide range of containers is an important asset to the flower arranger. This shallow shell dish with a little cherub perched at one end is in fact a soap dish! The flowers are short in the stem so just the stem tips are threaded through a small ball of wire netting held under the cherub's feet.

LEFT	BELOW
Scabious	*Anemone* 'The Bride'
Salvia	*Gentiana sino-ornata*
Aster	*Rosa* 'Cecile Brunner'
Ageratum	*Eucalyptus*
Crambe	*Cineraria*
Chrysanthemum 'Crystal'	
Senecio cineraria	
Eucalyptus	

RIGHT

This arrangement was created to fit neatly on a mirrored window sill. The stems, arranged in a block of Oasis standing in a flat dish, flow from a centre point following the lines of the walls.

FAR RIGHT

It is always important to arrange flowers in relation to their setting. Here there is a strong Chinese influence so a papier-mâché Chinese bowl (with a metal lining) contains a few exotic materials such as the swan plant, which resembles bamboo foliage.

BELOW

This small arrangement of Autumn greens in a china shell vase shows up some of the many different shapes available in materials at this time of year. The pretty calyx of cobaea can be used after the bell-shaped flower has fallen and it is very long-lasting.

RIGHT
Molucella
Lonicera
Helianthus

BELOW
Cobaea scandens
Symphoricarpos
Euonymus
Tellima
Hedera
Polygonum

FAR RIGHT
Amaryllis
Bergenia
Sedum
Paeonia (foliage)
Asclepias physocarpa

ABOVE

The pompom, single and cactus varieties of dahlias are grouped together here to give a splash of colour in a dark area at the foot of a staircase. Having such large flower heads, dahlias tend to make arrangements look rather heavy so here sloe foliage and some dahlia buds are used to help lighten the group.

RIGHT ABOVE

This two-arm pottery candlestick makes a good table centre for a rectangular table. It holds two aluminium candlecups which have been painted to match the candlestick. A small amount of netting has been placed in each, and for extra security the netting is taped to the candlecups with Oasis tape, as some of the materials used are quite heavy and could make the arrangement topple.

RIGHT

An all-round arrangement of mixed anemones is bright and colourful. This arrangement was made from two small bunches (twenty-four stems) and as there were only a few white flowers these have been grouped together to make them show up to advantage. Note the fact that no two flowers of the same length are next to each other and that some are placed deep down in the centre of the arrangement. Most of the greenery comes from the feathery collars of the anemones.

Anemones are normally at their best during the Autumn, Winter and Spring but their quality is very dependent on the weather. During a wet cold spell they can be short in the stem, their petals are often damaged and they do not last well when cut. Limp flowers can often be revived with a little hot water.

ABOVE
Dahlia
Prunus spinosa

RIGHT ABOVE
Rubus
Sambucus
Cobaea scandens
Rosa 'Carol'
Colchicum
Astrantia
Hedera

RIGHT
Anemone
Hedera
Eucalyptus

Zinnias are one of those flowers which look best arranged on their own with just a little foliage to give the arrangement some shape. The foliage of zinnia itself is rather un-interesting so here Autumn-tinted azalea and osmanthus foliage is used.

This group of baby zinnias in a copper jelly mould makes a striking arrangement on a shining brass table top. The large-flowered zinnias can be difficult to arrange as they sometimes bend over just below the flower head and may need supporting with a wire up the hollow stem.

If you have just a few of a particularly interesting material it is often best to use them on their own rather than in a mixed arrangement. The full beauty of these five hybrid nerine shows up well in this tall arrangement. Nerine are rarely picked with their own foliage so here black water grass was used to give the required height and lightness, and as the grass is light it will not upset the balance of the tall cylinder vase. A couple of trails of ivy hide the small ball of netting at the top of the vase and enhance the flow of the arrangement.

RIGHT

This elegant arrangement gives a good show of Autumn colour. The height is made from a single stem of atriplex and is linked to the rest of the group by many stems of various shades of kniphofia and a few salpiglossis in bronze shades. Dahlias and roses give weight to the vase and megasea leaves link the flowers to the container. Note the way the kniphofia have taken up flowing lines in water.

ABOVE
Nerine
Hedera
Gramineae

LEFT
Zinnia
Azalea
Osmanthus

RIGHT
Atriplex hortensis rubra
Kniphofia
Salpiglossis
Dahlia
Rosa 'Vesper'
Rosa 'Brownie'
Megasea
Tricholaena rosea

Very little foliage has been used in this simple collection of yellow garden flowers in order to make the group show up well against the dark background.

BELOW

This bright flower group stands on a wall table in a hallway, striking a cheerful note of welcome. It is arranged in an Oasis tray and picks up the colour and texture of the wallpaper. The flowers used are quite simple but the strength of colour is greater for the lack of green foliage—in fact a few rose leaves are the only green leaves in the arrangement. The roses and antirrhinums have been carefully placed at the centre to give weight to the arrangement.

LEFT
Lilium 'Destiny'
Rudbeckia
Antirrhinum
Helianthus
Alstroemeria
Gladiolus
Kniphofia
Solidago
Hedera
Achillea

BELOW
Statice sinuata
Solidago
Antirrhinum
Gladiolus
Atriplex
Amaranthus caudatus
 'Viridis'
Rosa 'Golden Showers'

Winter

November sees the end of most of the colour in the garden and it is always a shame that the last blossoms tend to go over very quickly in the warmth of a heated house. But there are many interesting materials available during the Winter months if only one looks carefully around—the first flowers of *Jasminum nudiflorum*, the buds of *Helleborus orientalis* tucked deeply in the foliage, and the early *Narcissus* 'Paper White' and *N.* 'Soleil d'Or' appear in the flower shops.

USEFUL MATERIALS
Berberis, Cotoneaster, Chrysanthemum (from florist), *Erica, Ilex, Mahonia, Narcissus* (from florist), *Prunus subhirtilla autumnalis, Pyracantha, Viburnum fragrans.*

December can be a very colourful month inside the home but the garden tends to be less so. Many of the berries will be lost to the birds and the flower arranger must look to the different shapes and tones of green in plant materials, instead of relying on colour from flowers. Artificial materials are often introduced at Christmas time and can be very attractive if used thoughtfully, following the usual principles of arrangement.

USEFUL MATERIALS
Arbutus unedo, Garrya elliptica, Helleborus niger, Hyacinthus, Iris stylosa, Jasminum nudiflorum, Viburnum fragrans.

SPECIAL CHRISTMAS MATERIALS
Cedrus atlantica glauca, Elaegnus aureo variegata, Hedera, Ilex, Picea pungens, Taxus baccata, Tsuga canadensis, Viscum album.

January is usually still a sparse time for garden flowers and only a few hardy ones will venture out. However, the change of seasons does vary greatly year by year, depending on the weather, and in some years in the south a camellia may be in full flower by mid-January.

USEFUL MATERIALS
Azalea, Corylus, Eranthis hyemalis, Galanthus nivalis, Hamamelis mollis, Hyacinthus, Iris unguicularis stylosa, Narcissus (from florist), *Salix caprea.*

February can be another difficult month but more and more flowers are available in the shops and these can be happily supplemented by garden foliages.

USEFUL MATERIALS
Alnus, Chimonanthus fragrans, Cornus mas, Crocus, Forsythia, Pieris floribunda, Syringa (from florist), *Tulipa, Viburnum opulus sterile* (from florist).

PAGES 98–9
Winter need not be a scant time for arrangements in the home. All the foliage and berries used in the arrangement on the previous page were found growing wild in the hedgerow in December.

ABOVE
Winter jasmine flowers throughout the Winter and here the first few stems are grouped with those other useful Winter materials, viburnum and alder.

A stem of alder, cut and placed in water, will easily last for two months indoors and the catkins will grow and become very decorative. The bare branches just lightly covered with glitter can also make a useful Christmas decoration.

RIGHT
Large chrysanthemum blooms are one of the few flowers readily available from florists during the Winter months and it is often difficult to use a small bunch of these. Here just five flowers are simply arranged. A stem of alder fitted to a pinholder makes the height and two side shoots form the width.

PAGES 98–9
Crataegus oxycantha
Symphoricarpos
Rosa canina
Ligustrum vulgare
Rhamnus cathartica
Euonymus europaeus
Hedera
Mahonia

ABOVE
Jasminum nudiflorum
Myrtus
Alnus
Viburnum fragrans

RIGHT
Chrysanthemum 'Yellow Indianapolis'
Aucuba japonica
Alnus

LEFT

A useful Winter arrangement can be made from small pieces of many different garden foliages. This type of mixed green arrangement does not call for particular materials to be grouped together or for one material to flow through the group. Instead, the aim should be to get different shapes and colours next to each other to enable each piece to show to good advantage.

RIGHT

Another useful and long-lasting arrangement for the Winter can be made using houseplants grouped purposefully together in a trough. Often a collection of houseplants is just thrown together without any thought given to the normal principles of flower arrangement, concerning, for example, the height and width of the arrangement and the shape of the individual materials.

BELOW LEFT

This special arrangement of flowers in a number of different shades of pink makes an attractive display in a handsome silver dolphin container. The flowers and berries flow beautifully through the arrangement and the nerine in particular makes a glorious sweep of colour through the centre. The bowl of this container is rather shallow and only holds a small glass container so it needs constant filling. Where the size of the stems in an arrangement permits, the use of a block of Oasis could help overcome this problem.

RIGHT

Wooden boxes can make superb containers for a special flower arrangement, particularly if the inside of the lid is decorative and can be featured. Here, because an antique tea caddy is used, the box is lined with polythene for extra security so no water marks will occur to spoil the box, then a bread tin is placed inside to hold the water. The tin holds a ball of wire netting in the usual way.

The flowers have been arranged in a low flowing way so that the beauty and detail of the box, including the leather cover on the inside of the lid, can be seen clearly.

LEFT	RIGHT
Nerine	*Rosa* 'Baccara'
Dianthus	*Rosa* 'Garnet'
Cynara	*Rosa* 'Mercedes'
Beta	*Rosa canina* and *R. gallica* (hips)
Rosa 'Carol'	
Astrantia	*Crataegus oxycantha*
Senecio	*Nerine*
Cineraria	*Dianthus* 'William Sim'
Potentilla	*Fagus*
Euonymus	
Pennisetum	

LEFT
Hedera
Tradescantia
Hosta
Polyanthus
Azalea

FAR LEFT
Ilex
Mahonia
Osmanthus
Phlomis
Senecio
Ruta
Rosmarinus
Cotoneaster
Veronica
Nephrolepsis
Cupressus
Hedera

LEFT
The first Christmas roses from the garden are often very short stemmed and in many cases the blooms have been damaged by the Winter weather conditions, but they make a pleasing Winter arrangement combined with holly, ivy and pine. To prevent frost and pest damage, cover the plants with a cloche as the buds appear and place peat or ashes around the plants.

BELOW
Hyacinths last well and fill the room with fragrance when growing as a pot plant or as a cut flower. These early white ones have been arranged in a flat copper dish with a few stems of 'Paper White' narcissi, hellebores and mixed Winter foliages consisting of pine, ivy trails and berries.

RIGHT
This arrangement in a cherub vase has been made up from washable silk flowers. Silk flowers are easy to arrange and give a fairly natural appearance. It is important to choose the colours carefully and to grade the shapes and sizes just as one would do when arranging fresh flowers.

In this group it is possible to pick out spray carnations, variegated ivy, small roses, eucalyptus, and a form of petunia.

ABOVE
Helleborus niger
Hedera
Pinus

RIGHT
Hyacinthus
Narcissus
  'Paper White'
Helleborus
Pinus
Hedera

ABOVE

Branches covered with lichen are useful in Winter when flowers are scarce and expensive. They make a delightful framework for just a few large blooms and the green-grey colourings go well with pink and mauve chrysanthemums arranged in pewter. Lichen is a fungus which develops on dead or dying branches and will only grow in very wet conditions. It develops on many types of trees in old neglected orchards and deciduous woodlands. When not in use, the branches, which are very brittle, should be stored carefully in a damp atmosphere. If the fungi do become dry, they can usually be brought back into good condition by soaking in a bath of lukewarm water.

Bracket fungi and any other forms of lichen on stone and wood can be used from time to time. They will keep well if stored carefully but will not grow if kept dry.

Lichen on branches is occasionally available in flower shops although you should always keep an eye open for it when travelling around the countryside. You should be able to pick up beautifully shaped branches that would probably never come to market because of the difficulty of transporting them.

Another rather pretty decoration which is easily made for the Winter time, when fresh flowers are in short supply, is made with elegant sprays of larch, magnolia or lime branches and if they have some lichen on them so much the better. To give the branches a little highlight, first lightly varnish them, then, with a quick-drying glue, attach very small helichrysum or immortelle flowers to the stem in clusters. This will give the appearance of little blossoms on the branches. Allow them to dry thoroughly and arrange them in a suitable container. The secret is to work very carefully with your glue so the stems do not look messy. I like to see these stems in an oriental-style container, and they can be fixed onto an old pinholder, held firmly with some decorative stones. This is more attractive than many decorations on sale before Christmas.

Driftwood is used mostly as an accessory, although it can be the basis of a complete arrangement. At the Flower School we rarely use it but it is attractive when carefully chosen.

Some florists will sell pieces of driftwood, but they seldom have just the piece you are looking for. If you often use driftwood, keep pieces fixed permanently to bases and then you can add the flowers each time to complete the picture.

Driftwood is found at the side of lakes or on the sea shore where it has been brought up by the tide. Interesting shaped branches are also occasionally found in woodland areas where branches and sometimes trees have died and eventually fallen. It is best to make a collection of pieces from which to choose the necessary shape, as it takes a very sharp eye to select the right piece.

Driftwood can be used in its natural form, which blends in very well with flowers and plant materials, or it can be polished by sanding it down to a really smooth surface and applying a stain polish or varnish. Some people use it in a bleached form which can be obtained by soaking it in a household bleach for a day or so before drying and polishing.

The choice of materials and the selection of the correct piece of driftwood calls for great artistic ability and I admire some of the work which I have seen, but I do not like to see a lot of wood at the expense of flowers. I was once asked to judge a competition entitled 'Use of wood'. Some of the entries had so much wood that it was more like a forest scene than a flower show!

Polished offcuts of wood make excellent bases for some arrangements, especially those in Autumn colourings or when dried materials have been used.

In this arrangement are two pieces of pine roots washed by the waves at the lakeside over many years. They were fixed in the trough with plasticine and the other materials are arranged in a pinholder and netting.

ABOVE
Narcissus
Garrya eliptica
Hedera

Decorating a Christmas tree

If possible, choose a tree with evenly spaced branches, and prune out any short bushy stems on the main trunk before decorating it. This gives more space to display the decorations and prevents the finished effect from looking heavy. The tree in this photograph was nailed to a silver birch log: a firm base is most important, particularly if there are children around, as a tree that is not securely anchored will topple over easily. If the tree has roots, it can be potted into a large clay flower pot or wooden tub. Place several bricks or stones in the pot with the soil or sand to give added weight and support.

Fairy lights, if used, should be put on first. Space them out evenly over the tree and try to ensure that they do not run in lines or rings around the branches. Fasten the light wires to the branches with short pieces of florist's wire or green string. For this tree a colour scheme of green and gold was chosen to harmonize with the colour scheme in the room. Unless one is decorating a very large tree, it is usually more effective to stick to one or two colours for the trimmings.

The star at the top of this tree was fixed in position after the lights were secured. Gold and green bows and streamers were added to make a strong bold topknot. Large bows of similar ribbon decorate the base and help to hide the light flex where it is not hidden under the carpet. The fairy was then placed in a prominent position where the branches were rather sparse.

To achieve a feeling of weight down the centre of the tree, use some of the bolder decorations close to the main trunk, keeping the lighter and smaller pieces to the outside. Colours should be roughly balanced out over the whole tree, keeping most of the darker and heavier trimmings towards the base. Where baubles or bells are used, they are attached either singly or in clusters, using a ribbon bow to hold them in place. Garlands of tinsel on a Christmas tree often have the effect of dividing it into sections and hiding the other decorations. One of the prettiest ways of using tinsel is to take short lengths and hang baubles or bells from them, and this will give an added sparkle to the overall effect of the tree.

ABOVE This 'partridge in a pear tree' decoration can be made at home quite simply.

RIGHT In common with other types of arrangement, a Christmas tree should be decorated with care and thought.

Partridge in a pear tree

Cut out 35 leaves from a sheet of lurex paper. Cover 35 stem wires with fine strips of green crêpe paper and attach one to the back of each leaf with adhesive tape. Trim off any excess tape with scissors so that none is showing from the front. The leaves can be tooled with a heated tooling iron to give a textured surface. Cover the crêpe paper on the stems with 5 mm ($\frac{1}{4}$ inch) wide strips of gold crinkle paper. Paint three plastic pears with gold paint. The base of the tree is made from plasterer's cement mixed with a little water to a stiff consistency. When dry it is painted with gold paint. The little partridge, bought from a shop, is attached by its wired feet.

Plastic maidenhair fern tree

Take all the individual branchlets off the main stems of two large pieces of plastic maidenhair fern and attach a florist's stem wire to each branchlet. Varnish each fern spray and sprinkle with silver glitter. Make a stem for each of the pine cones with reel wire, varnish them and sprinkle on a mixture of gold and green glitter.

Attach one cone to each of the fern sprays by twisting the finer wire round the heavier one.

Cover the wires with narrow strips of green crêpe paper cut on the bias. Start binding the wires of the branchlets together with fine wire to form the top of the main stem, working down the stem.

Cover the stem with crêpe paper strips, hiding each wire as it is added. Gradually make bigger branches by joining three sprays together. This widens the tree as it nears the base.

Incorporate some extra plain wires to thicken the main stem and give extra support to the increasing weight.

When all the branches have been added, bind the remaining stem firmly with crêpe paper, fastening the end down with glue.

Bend out a few wires at the bottom and make a base with plasterer's cement, mixed to a stiff consistency.

When thoroughly dry, paint the base and shape the branches into a natural tree form.

The more natural you can make the arrangement, the more effective and attractive it will be.

BELOW RIGHT Waterlily with a tinsel candle table decoration.

BELOW Plastic maidenhair fern tree.

Waterlily with tinsel candle

Cut out eight large leaf shapes and five smaller leaf shapes from a double thickness of heavy white net. Keep the shapes in pairs. Cover thirteen thin florist's wires with narrow bias strips of white crêpe paper. Using a clear glue, stick a covered wire down the centre of one leaf, and then stick on the corresponding half. Brush glue round the edge and along the central vein and sprinkle on some fine gold glitter.

Cut some stiff red paper into three feathers, making a series of scissor cuts. With adhesive tape attach both this and the end of a long strip of tinsel to the top of a firm wire. Twist the tinsel round the wire until it is thickly covered. Fill a glass candle-holder with white plasticine and press in first the tinsel candle, then the wires of the eight large leaves, and finally make an inner ring with the five smaller leaves.

Table centre with mistletoe

The sprays of mistletoe are made first. Make a cardboard template of the leaf pattern and trace it on the back of some green crinkle paper which has been folded in half.

When enough leaves have been traced, cut them out through the double thickness of paper and place them in pairs with the green surfaces facing the table. Cover the back of one leaf with glue and then lay a thin florist's wire along the leaf. Press the corresponding half leaf onto the glued piece and leave it to dry.

When all the leaves are made up, thread some imitation pearl beads onto wires. Hold a pair of the leaves around each berry and bind the three wires together firmly with thin strips of the green paper. Outline the sprays of plastic ivy and holly with clear varnish and sprinkle gold glitter over them while the varnish is wet.

Press plasticine around the base of the candle to fill the candleholder. Press the ends of the leaf sprays firmly into the plasticine and spread them out to the desired shape. The bows are made from wire-edged red ribbon and are inserted on short wires at the base of the candle to hide any plasticine which is still showing around the base.

Robin on a standard holly tree

Mount twelve clusters of artificial plastic holly onto 30 cm (12 inch) heavy gauge florist's wires. Cover each wire separately with 1 cm ($\frac{1}{3}$ inch) wide strips of green crêpe paper cut on the bias. Attach the robin's feet to a 30 cm (12 inch) wire and cover this with crêpe paper.

Holding the holly stems and the robin wire in a bunch, firmly bind them all together at a point about 7·5 cm (3 inches) below the leaves. Cover the remainder of the long wires with crêpe paper: this forms the stem of the tree.

Spray a small plastic pot with gold paint. Put a little plasticine in the bottom to hold the stem of the tree in position. Then spoon in enough plasterer's cement mixed with water to almost fill the pot.
When it has set firmly and dried out (about 24 hours) paint it with some clear varnish and sprinkle glitter on top while the varnish is still wet.

When completely dry, bend the holly clusters outwards to form a ball shape, making sure that the robin is at the top. Attach two bows of ribbon at the top of the stem where the branches join and leave the loose ends to hang down towards the pot.

ABOVE Table centre with mistletoe (left) and robin on a standard holly tree decoration.

111

Flowers
for children

PAGES 112–3 The maypole for this children's party was made by plaiting ribbon round a pole. A piece of Oasis holds the pole and the flowers (*Dianthus* and *Lathyrus* with *Ruta* foliage).
BELOW *Centaurea* in a small plastic pot covered with nursery-rhyme wrapping paper, and *Viola* and *Adiantum* in an eggshell fixed to a plaster of paris base, with lichen and cones set into it.

Most young children love flowers; I have often watched their faces light up with excitement when they find themselves among flowers, either wild or cultivated ones. This interest should be fostered so they gradually appreciate the beauty of flowers, and they should be encouraged to put them in water and watch them grow.

I can still remember receiving, while in hospital at the age of six or seven, a small pot of grape hyacinths beautifully mossed up. These had been bought so that they could be planted in my own little garden when I got home. What a disappointment it was to find that they were not bulbs at all but that the florist has used cut flowers and just stuck them in damp sand covered with moss!

Containers for children's arrangements can be quite small, and a lot of interesting improvisations can be made. An eggshell could, for example, make a useful container.

Carefully remove the top from a hard-boiled egg without cracking the basal part and remove the contents: a free-range egg will normally have a harder shell. Fill the egg with moist Florapak or damp sand and stand it in a napkin ring or a base made from plaster of paris. Into this can be placed a small posy of wild flowers or some of the small garden flowers such as the baby-rose 'Cecile Brunner', forget-me-nots, fine grasses, gypsophila and flowers from the rock garden.

A jam jar or honey pot can make an excellent flower holder. Fix the pot to a firm circular base of wood or stick a piece of felt to it, then make a covering by glueing pieces of bark and any other interesting material together to hide the container. Cork oak from Portugal is useful as it is very light and easy to work with.

A jar can also be papered with a coarse reeded or Japanese straw paper, but the

paper should not get spotted with water because some papers stain easily. An ordinary tin which holds water could be used in this way too, but first check that it has no raw or jagged edges as these can be very dangerous. A coat of paint inside and out will stop it rusting.

There are many kinds of sea shell available today and they can be most attractive filled with simple flowers. Make certain that they will not leak to avoid damaging the furniture. If the shell does not stand well of its own accord, make a plaster of paris base and fix the shell to it. This base can be painted when dry and a piece of felt can be stuck on the underside to finish off the surface and prevent it scratching. Simplicity is important and over-arranging will spoil the effect.

A small basket with a metal lining (a baking tin is ideal) can be most attractive with mixed garden flowers. For a little extra detail, a frill of chintz or gingham in blue or red can be added round the basket, tied on with a drawstring, and the handle covered with the same material.

A log with its base levelled but still retaining the rest of its bark, may be hollowed out in the top to hold a block of Oasis; the base should be painted with pitch and a piece of felt glued to it so that no moisture will filter through to spoil the furniture that it will stand on. Natural wood is ideal for simple flowers of yellow, cream, orange and rust colourings, and a silver birch log looks good with silver-grey foliages and pale shades of pink, mauve and blue.

Although there are no specific rules to follow when arranging flowers for children, the most important thing to bear in mind is that the arrangement should be simple but interesting. The container can play a large part in the charm of the finished arrangement but, as always, the main thing is to choose the plant materials carefully and then let them speak for themselves.

ABOVE A small hamper basket is brightened up with a frill of yellow ribbon and contains *Freesia* and *Hypericum* (in both flower and berry).

115

ABOVE A miniature
basket with wild
Clematis and side
shoots of
Chrysanthemum
'Crystal'. A shell on
its side holds *Zinnia*
and *Berberis* in a
small piece of Oasis.

A miniature garden, such as the special Easter garden illustrated on the facing page can easily be made by children without going to a lot of expense, as any small wild or garden flowers are suitable. The scheme can be arranged on a fairly wide window ledge, or on a flat board or wooden tray.

First cover the surface with tin foil, waxed paper or fairly strong polythene and on this place little containers to hold the flowers. Aerosol tops or the bases of plastic drinking beakers make ideal pots, or anything else that is about 5 cm (2 inches) deep and the same width across.

For the taller groups of flowers very small pinholders are useful but you can use a small ball of wire netting and put some silver sand in the container. This will weight it down and keep the main stems upright. Silver sand is cleaner than builder's sand.

Collect pieces of moss and lichen to add interest. Bun moss—the thick clumps found growing on roofs and walls—is excellent to place between pieces of stone and bark and will quickly cover the surface around the water pots. Before using bun moss, soak it well to drive out any insects and worms that may be hidden in it. If you buy it from a florist, it may well have been packed in kipper boxes to bring it to market, so will smell very strongly of fish until well soaked and

allowed to drain in the open.

All the flowers to be used should be given the correct treatment to make them last (see Care and handling of cut flowers). Group them into colours and different shapes and decide on a plan as you would for any arrangement; in fact you are doing many small simple arrangements. Fix the height first with some foliage or a slender flower, then set the width with other leaves or flowers and fill in between, getting plenty of variation of length, never putting two flowers the same length next to each other.

Once you have completed the first group, move to the next, working along the line of pots. The number of groups and how they are placed will vary with the size of the base; do not overcrowd them, but allow each group of flowers to show up clearly.

The shorter flowers, such as primroses, double daisies and little violets can be carefully tied into bunches with elastic bands and placed in little clumps towards the front if the garden is to be seen only from there.

Once the garden is set up, moss up around the stone, rock and tree bark, then top up the containers. Do not allow the moss to syphon off the water: this will happen if it is put too close to the pot rim or if the pot is too full of water. The whole area should be sprayed over to help the flowers last and keep the moss green. Top up the pots each day or more often if necessary.

A 'garden' can be used for a table decoration or a low coffee table instead of a vase arrangement but it will only look well on a polished surface. First place a strip of waxed paper down the centre of the table and position the pots at irregular stations, not in one straight line.

The best time of year to do these arrangements is in spring, from the first snowdrops in January right through until about mid-May in the North of England. They can be made up from one flower such as snowdrops, but the wealth of colour and the different shapes of all the small spring flowers really are ideal.

Useful plants for miniature gardens

Allium	*Jasminum*	BELOW A miniature
Anemone	*Muscari*	garden made in
Chimonanthus	*Myosotis*	Spring, and
Crocus	*Petasites*	containing *Salix,*
Eranthis	*Primula*	*Narcissus* 'Silver
Erica	*Prunus spinosa*	Chimes', *Allium,*
Forsythia	*Pulmonaria*	*Forsythia,*
Freesia	*Ranunculus*	*Cheiranthus,*
Galanthus	*Salix*	*Laurustinus,*
Gentiana	*Scilla nutans*	*Anemone, Fritillaria*
Hedera	*Tulipa*	*meleagris, Primula,*
Helleborus	*Tussilago farfara*	*Muscari,*
Hyacinthus	*Viburnum*	*Hyacinthus,*
Iris reticulata	*Viola*	*Myosotis.*

Special arrangements

1

2

3

4

Large groups

Do the arrangement in the permanent position as a large arrangement cannot be moved. A bowl is by far the best container to stand on a pedestal as it allows the maximum amount of room for stems and when filled with water is fairly heavy and will sit well on the pedestal. To add extra weight, tie something heavy on the netting at the back of the bowl, or even two blocks of Oasis placed well towards the back. A little extra care when setting up the container will be well repaid in the long run.

If the materials are short in the stem, it will help to work with flower cones set up on square stakes and firmly fixed into the netting. Five or seven is the usual number to use but this will depend on the overall finished size. The stakes can be painted dark green, but if the flowers are well arranged no cones or stakes should show. Proportion between flowers and vase is of the utmost importance and although one cannot lay down rules, I think that arranging the flowers in the following way will help.

⚓ As usual, first fix the background foliage. This should be trimmed and shaped to give a pleasing effect and should be placed at least two-thirds of the way towards the back of the vase, leaning back very slightly. If many flowers are to go into the vase, place the background foliage right at the back, but allow for the curve of the container wall. Stand well back at this stage to see that you have the correct height and change it now if necessary, because once flowers are added it will be impossible to take out the background foliage. It is important to get the correct proportion and only your own taste and experience will guide you here.

⚓ Next, set the width to the arrangement, choosing shapely pieces (trimming to exaggerate a curve will help), anchoring the stems under the netting at the back of the vase. If Oasis is being used, set them firmly into this.

⚓ When the outline is settled, stand well back once again to see the overall picture. Your flowers may go to the outline but should never extend beyond it.

⚓ The flower cones or tubes are the next to go in, the fewer the better. Fill them with water and put a small piece of netting in each.

⚓ At this stage it is a good idea to fix some foliage over the rim of the vase at the front to link the flowers and vase together.

⚓ Next get your main centre flowers in position. They will probably be large blooms, such as lilies. Then place the smaller flowers carefully in the cones, setting them through the group in sweeps of colour and shapes.

Each particular bloom or special leaf should show up well and all the stems should appear to flow from the centre of the vase. A little foliage should go between the stakes of the cones to disguise them.

⚓ Bring the flowers well out over the front to give the group a three-dimensional effect and to avoid the surprised look of flowers appearing to leap out of the vase: there should be no hard rim showing. Some material should be well recessed to give weight and depth to the group, and this will help the balance. Make use of the flower buds and half-open flowers, using the fully open blooms lower down. The balance of the arrangement should be both actual and visual.

⚓ If the group has to look very large and is more than a facing arrangement, place one or two flowers either side of the centre, facing back from the group to give it more of an all round effect.

ABOVE A large green and white group of stripped lime, *Hosta glauca*, *Alchemilla*, *Lilium* 'Regale', *Rosa alba maxima* and *R.* 'Iceberg'.

LEFT Four steps to a pedestal arrangement containing *Phormium*, *Alnus*, *Prunus lusitanica*, *Chrysanthemum* 'Ray', *Lilium* 'Destiny', *Alstroemeria*, *Gladiolus*, *Dianthus*, *Rosa* 'Evergold', *Arbutus*.
PAGES 118–9 *Freesia* flowers, buds and side shoots with *Eucalyptus* foliage.

There is a tendency to overcrowd arrangements because of the fear of the mechanics showing, but an extra leaf or a recessed flower may be enough to hide the netting.

When light feathery materials are used, the stems may be twice the length of those on heavy blooms. Dense colours make materials appear heavier so they must be on shorter stems to look right.

Avoid over-arranging, especially with simple garden materials. It is difficult to be logical about matters of taste—choosing the right material and vase is important, but only *you* can decide what these should be, with the setting in mind. Remember that the background is part of the composition and arrange the group where it is to be displayed.

Remember that flowers may well overbalance as they open and cause large arrangements to topple. This reminds me of an occasion when a very happy day could have ended in just such a disaster. Three of us had gone to Sussex to arrange the flowers for a big wedding—the church, the house and the marquee—and it was all to be in stripped lime, lilies and peonies. The church was so small that only a few flowers would be required in each group to make a big display. One of the places chosen for a group was up above the back of the altar in the little side chapel, a very difficult spot to reach. We borrowed a large pair of steps and luckily there was a fair-sized flat area on which to place the large baking tin that we were using as the container. One of the team stood at a distance and gave directions on size and shape, and the second person held the steps while I placed the flowers in the container—quite a precarious operation!

The lime went in easily and a few large leaves 'broke' the hard rim of the tin and linked the flowers and container together. The lilies then went in and lastly the peony buds—not many, but just enough to give a touch of pink. We carefully topped up the vase with water and opened the fanlight in the old glass window behind the altar.

As is always our practice, the next day we visited the church to see that all was well and to top up the vases and cones. To our horror we found that the vase above the altar had fallen, the altar was soaked with water, and the blue dye of the altar frontal had run into the starched white overmantle! The opening peonies had tipped the balance. We learned our lesson and now weight down containers when using heavy flowers that flow well over the container rim.

A tied bunch

This is a useful and attractive way of presenting flowers as a gift. The materials should have a good drink before tying. Select a fairly long straight stem for the back of the bunch. Fix the string to this, a little way from the tip of the stem. Tie in one or two more stems, holding the bunch in one hand and positioning the pieces with the other hand. Continue in this way, adding a little at a time, paying particular attention to colours, shapes and length of materials as in all arrangements. The bunch should have fullness at the front. Finish off with a collar of leaves and a neat decorative bow.

Font decorations

When the font is used for a christening, the flowers should always be a special feature. They can be done in various ways. A florist will measure the circumference of the font and make a frame to fit it. This will be covered with bun moss or flower heads and groups of flowers will be wired at three or five stations around the frame. The main group is in the centre, with one or two smaller groups on either side, and the flowers should hang down over the edge of the font in the form of a shower. The colourings will be in white and green, with blue or pink added, or may be in all pastel shades. Allow plenty of flower-free space at the back of the font for the vicar. It is important that the flowers are not so high that they hide the baby from the view of the congregation.

A person not trained in floristry may arrange flowers in a different way but they can still be effective. If there is a good ledge around the font, small containers can be placed on it and these can be linked with trails of ivy to disguise them and link them together. Place little posies of flowers in these small pots and you will have a charming setting for a christening. If there is no large rim on which to stand little containers, make do with the trails of ivy, which can easily be fixed with a waterproof tape; then place a garland around the base of the font with the flowers standing on the floor. This is attractive when seen from a distance but is not so effective during the service, as all the colour is hidden.

Fonts may also be decorated at other times. Never arrange flowers directly in the font, although it may be possible to get a large bowl to fit into it to take an all-round arrangement. Some fonts have a heavy flat wooden cover—if this is turned upside down, a bowl or large vase can stand on it to take the arrangement. A stone-coloured, old-fashioned mixing bowl is ideal.

For Easter, the font can be treated as for a christening; but with the flowers all the way round. Small flowers like primroses, Roman hyacinths, polyanthus and grape hyacinths will be excellent tucked in thick moss.

At Christmas, use little clusters of holly and berries, variegated and plain groups, mistletoe, pine with cones, and one or two small groups of red flowers, all linked together with ivy trails.

At Harvest Festival use trails of hops between the posies of flowers and, again, use berries, fruits and flowers.

FACING PAGE Four steps to a tied bunch. BELOW A heavy-looking font calls for larger arrangements than usual. Here the mixed flowers are arranged in Oasis bowls and the areas between arrangements are linked with *Ruta* foliage.

Church arrangements

The general principles of flower arranging also apply to church groups but there are just a few specific points to bear in mind. Always use a strong background foliage to throw the colours of the flowers forward. This is particularly important if blue and mauve colourings are to be used as these are easily lost against stone walls. Although the groups may be large, keep the overall lines of the arrangement quite simple and use a few large flowers in preference to many small ones which will be lost from a distance.

LEFT Harvest colours are traditionally the golden Autumn shades, but here reds, purples, and pinks are based around an artichoke and an aubergine. Sprays of black-berries blend with *Antirrhinum*, *Zinnia*, *Chrysanthemum*, *Hydrangea* and *Sedum*.
BELOW Arrangements at Easter-time often feature *Narcissus*. This church arrangement also includes *Salix*, *Forsythia*, *Berberis* *japonica*, *Euphorbia*, *Tulipa*, and *Hedera*.
RIGHT BELOW A church window ledge is a good site for an arrangement, as the flowers are in full view yet well out of the way. This harvest festival arrangement shows off a collection of Autumnal fruits and vegetables. The flowers include *Rosa* 'Peace', *Lilium* 'Destiny', *Coton-easter*, *Azalea*, *Paeonia*, *Dahlia*, *Gladiolus*, *Chrysanthemum*, *Helianthus*.

LEFT An Easter arrangement made up of ten arum lilies and some wild cherry with *Megasea* and *Prunus lusitanica* foliage.

RIGHT This Christmas group of foliages and flowers could be seen at any time of year if it were not for the berries. The height is fixed with the bare wood of *Cornus* and long stems of *Rosmarinus*. *Senecio, Elaeagnus, Eucalyptus, Laurus* and *Ceanothus* are other foliages used, and the centre is a head of *Mahonia bealei*. Berries of *Mahonia gagnepainii, Ilex* and *Hedera* give interest, and the unusual form of *Chrysanthemum* is 'Luyona'.

RIGHT Arranging flowers against a colourful or highly decorated background is always a problem. For this Christmas altar group white has been chosen to avoid any clash with the wonderful mosaic behind. The outline of the arrangement is made from *Salix caprea*, just showing silver flower buds, and *Cedrus atlantica glauca*. Variegated holly tends to be rather untidy in growth and these pieces needed some trimming for a good shape. *Fatsia japonica* leaves break the rim of the vase, and the chrysanthemums are 'American Beauty' and 'Bonnie Jean'.

LEFT This rich Christmas arrangement in seasonal colourings could either stand on its own at one side of the altar or be one of a pair. The berries are from two varieties of holly, rose hips, *Pyracantha* and tree ivy. The iris seed pods were picked in the Autumn and dried, and a few stems of larch bearing cones trail over the edge of the vase. Flowers are *Dianthus* 'William Sim' and an unknown spray carnation, and *Chrysanthemum*.

Wedding flowers

Wedding flowers create the setting for the wedding ceremony, suggesting a note of welcome to the guests before the arrival of the bride, but it is not a flower festival and the arrangements should not overshadow the beauty of the church itself.

As a general guide, for an average-sized church, six or eight arrangements of flowers would be suitable, and it is better to make prominent groups rather than have flowers dotted around everywhere. Simplicity is the key to success and a few large flowers in the centre of each of the groups will show to good advantage.

Each church will have its own likes and dislikes and it is important to get permission to carry out any decoration within the church. Some churches allow flowers on the altar, others prefer them behind the Holy Table or a group either side of it. Whenever possible, try to use the church's own vases because these are usually in keeping with the rest of the church furnishings.

The flowers at the altar should be simple and there is nothing better than some form of large lily, remembering that many different types of flowers do not show up well from a distance. It is traditional to use white at the altar, and a few well-arranged stems with some clear-cut foliages should be sufficient.

Two very large groups—in fact these are the main flower arrangements at the wedding —should stand on either side of the chancel rail, where they always show to good advantage, as the main part of the wedding service takes place here. These flowers may be all white or in colours which are linked to the bridal party colours. A lot will depend on the type of church and its wall colours; for instance, if decorating an old church which has grey stone walls inside, great care must be taken if using blue flowers, as they will fade into the background colour and be quite lost from a distance, giving the appearance of great gaps in the arrangements. To overcome this, see that a good foil of background green foliage is used to throw the flower colour forward. Some large simple flowers will help at the centre of these groups, for example one of the lilies or large blooms such as peonies, chrysanthemums or hydrangeas.

Another pair of smaller vases will look well standing on either side of the main aisle of the church. These will contain the same type of flowers as those at the chancel rails but should be on a smaller scale and often without the special centre flowers.

When arranging a pair of vases it is important to share the flowers carefully so that each vase has the same materials. It is easy to make one very nice arrangement and then find that there are too few flowers left to complete the other one. It may be that the position calls for identical or symmetrical arrangements, or two arrangements with flowing lines from left to right and right to left.

Whatever the chosen shapes, always set the height of each first, then the width. This can only be done by standing well back after each piece has been placed in position. Once you have the outline, work on the centre, taking care to see that the materials and colours are brought in sweeps rather than blocks of different colours or shapes. When working with really big groups it is important to have long flowing materials. No pleasing flow can be obtained by working with short materials in flower cones, although these aids are ideal for adding to the framework of the arrangement and getting extra amounts of colour or interest where needed.

If the church is to be full of people, consider the use of window ledges: these often prove troublesome because they slope and it is difficult to hold the container in place, but they are ideal positions for flowers, out

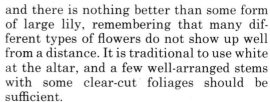

BELOW The altar group at an early Summer wedding in a small country church. The foliages are *Typha, Sorbus aria lutescens, Hosta sieboldiana, Bergenia cordifolia*, and the flowers are *Gladiolus, Euphorbia characias, Chrysanthemum* and *Antirrhinum*.

Bouquets

of the way, yet in full view of everyone. Many churches have overcome the difficulty by providing special platforms for the vases to stand on, and a low container such as a bread-baking tin would be ideal. To help balance it, some stone chippings should be placed in its base. Painted in a neutral stone colour, the container will not show when well arranged. For extra safety, fix a wire from the back of the container to the window frame.

A group at the back of the church is the last thing one sees on leaving after the service. A very nice idea is to have a group of flowers in the entrance porch of the church; a lantern vase hanging inside the porch roof can look very good and may well feature in the photography after the service if a group picture is taken just outside the church.

Flowers for the bride and her bridesmaids are almost as important as the dresses, and the colour and shape of the bouquets form an essential part of the general scheme. This work is carried out by the professional florist and no amateur should attempt it.

In planning a wedding it is well to remember that the procession down the aisle contains an element of pageantry so, although detail is important, a certain uniformity is necessary, and the greater the number of bridesmaids the more clearly this should be emphasized. It is important that the bridesmaids should, irrespective of their individuality, act as one and strive to make the wedding procession as beautiful, flowing and harmonious as possible.

ABOVE An arrangement in the Marquee. The vase, three cherubs holding up a bowl, is ideal to stand on a buffet as it raises the material well above the table. The materials are *Tellima, Eucalyptus, Chrysanthemum, Helleborus, Mahonia bealei, Hosta, Dianthus, Delphinium.*

The Reception

A clever photographer using the porch as a background may well include the flowers in the photograph to give it extra interest. Care must be taken, however, to see that any flower arrangements which are hanging from the roof do not appear to be growing out of the bridal couple's heads.

So often the wedding reception will take place in a marquee in the garden and nothing can be nicer if the weather is kind. On a hot summer's day the sides can be opened to bring in the garden as a bonus.

Marquees are not easy to decorate and it is very important to get the flowers well up so that they may be seen by everyone when all are gathered under the canvas. People spend hours garlanding poles with foliages and flowers but to my mind this is expensive both on flowers and time and, if not very well done, the result can be most disappointing. In any case, it always emphasises the poles which really want hiding as far as possible. The most successful way of decorating the marquee is to have baskets on chains hanging from the roof – one between each pole if chandeliers are not going to be used for lighting, or half baskets joined together and fixed well up on the poles. The poles are first covered with the lining material to make them less noticeable. In this way, large groups of lovely, flowing flowers appear right down the centre of the marquee which can be seen from all angles.

To get extra colour, half baskets can be hung from the poles along the sides of the marquee. They are especially suitable if a buffet table is going to be along one wall. These should be fixed at a height to allow a well balanced arrangement, remembering the sides of a marquee tend to be rather low.

Large free standing groups are not easy to do under canvas as they usually have to stand well into the body of the marquee to get the height to the group. This often wastes valuable space and may prove difficult to get really stable on a soft ground surface. Nothing is more embarrassing than to find a group of flowers go over because someone has brushed by in the rather confined space.

If large tables for 8 to 10 people are being used for a sit down breakfast, then each table can have its own flower arrangement. If only small occasional tables are being used my advice is to forget flowers on these. They are always in the way and once the food is brought round they are often relegated to the floor and wasted. A lot of thought and imagination can go into really artistic party flowers and the use of special clothes, napkins, candles and ribbons should all be colour co-ordinated.

The Church porch

Many of our old country churches have the most attractive porches yet these are seldom made a feature of unless it is a flower festival when every area available is filled with flowers.

On the occasion of a wedding, guests often gather around the porch before going in for the service. What nicer way is there of greeting them than with a cheerful group of flowers?

RIGHT:
Flowers always look well, are out of the way and can be seen by all when they are hanging in a marquee. This pretty metal hanging lantern is simply arranged in pink and white colourings to tie up with the bridal party. The foliages are *Eucalyptus*, *Cineraria maritima*, *Viburnum* and variegated ivy. The flowers consist of bridal pink and Carte Blanche roses, Tokyo *Chrysanthemum* spray, *Astrantia maxima* and spray carnations.

FAR RIGHT:
A most welcome sight greets one on reaching Cranbourne Church porch. This Autumnal group arranged in a large bowl could be used for any occasion. It contains *Chrysanthemum* blooms and spray. The main foliage backing is of *Viburnum tinus* with a bold centre of beautifully coloured *Mahonia japonica*. There are two kinds of berries used. The bright red are *Iris foetidissima* and the long arching sprays are *Celastrus*. Trails of *Hedera canariensis variegata* soften the outline around the base of the arrangement.

Dried flowers

ABOVE This little picture is made from small pieces of dried materials which one would normally throw out as being too small to use. The pieces have been joined together and then glued to the fabric before mounting and framing.

PAGES 132–3 This arrangement has been done in a small piece of Oasis which is fitted into a shallow shell. The shell rests on a brass twin dolphin base which came from a tray of oddments at a junk shop. The foliage is tips of *Eucalyptus* which have been placed in a solution of glycerine for a short while; all the other materials have been air-dried. The height of the vase is made from *Delphinium* and sprays of *Erica*. The other flowers are *Statice sinuata* and *Acroclinium*.

Towards the end of the year, when little is available from the garden, I like to make use of dried materials to help with flower decorations although, to my mind, nothing can take the place of a few fresh flowers.

Today there are many very real-looking plastic and other artificial flowers for special work such as in the theatre, but they cannot match real dried ones, which retain some of their original life and movement. With many dried flowers coming from abroad there is a wealth of material to use but the natural and bleached colourings are the most effective.

I prefer to use dried flowers in the late Autumn and Winter and store them for the Spring and Summer. They will keep over the years but they become brittle as they get older. It is important to keep them clean and free from dust, and when not in use, stored in boxes between sheets of tissue paper in a dry place. They will soon go mouldy if they become damp. You can store them in large plastic bags to which a little drying agent, such as silica gel, has been added, but keep natural coloured stems in the dark to prevent them fading. Remember also to keep an eye on them, because they are attractive to mice.

The range of materials which can be dried is vast and gives scope for many colour schemes. Trees and shrubs, roses, herbaceous plants, ferns and grasses all respond to drying. Dried materials can be divided into two main groups: flowers in bright colours which are harvested from the garden or bought in the early Autumn, and foliages and seed heads which tend to be more sombre in their brown-green colourings; both are useful. All

these materials can be used during the summer as fresh flowers and foliages so, if you have room to grow them in the garden, they serve a dual purpose.

It is most important to harvest at the correct time, and only perfect materials should be used if they are to dry properly and keep their character, although they always lose a little of their colour during the drying process. It is a waste of time to harvest and dry partially damaged or weathered materials because any marked tissue will tend to show up more distinctly as the drying takes place. Drying and preserving should be done straight after picking.

The art of drying and preserving is very skilled and makes a fascinating hobby, though it can be time-consuming and take up rather a lot of room if done in a big way. Some plant materials will dry well if hung upside down, or if covered with silica gel or borax and packed in boxes.

Many types of foliage such as beech, eucalyptus, hornbeam, stripped lime and oak, to name a few, can be preserved with a solution of glycerine and water in equal parts. Some people say that for the soft-leaved foliages one part glycerine to two parts water is quite sufficient, but the stronger or tougher the leaves, the stronger the solution needed. At the Constance Spry Flower School we always dry all foliages in a mixture of equal parts.

Dissolve the glycerine in near-boiling water. Stand the stems, not too many at a time, in a fairly deep container while the solution is still warm. There should be at least 15 cm (6 inches) of liquid covering the base of the stem. Glycerine is quite expensive, so if you propose to use a lot of it, it would be cheaper to buy the commercial type from a chemist. A glycerine-based anti-freeze can be used but some contain a dye which may discolour your material.

Carefully select well-shaped branches as it is pointless to treat pieces that will not be of use afterwards. Remove any damaged and unwanted shoots (these small pieces, if preserved in the same way, can be used to fill in an arrangement) and then hammer the base of the stem. If the bark is very thick, peel some off to show the white wood below (this will help it take up the glycerine solution). Be sure that the foliage is mature but not too advanced before commencing treatment, otherwise some of the leaves may fall before the glycerine is absorbed. Once Autumn colours have started to appear on the leaf, natural chemical changes have taken place and the supply of moisture to that leaf has been cut off so the glycerine will never reach it.

Allow the stems to stand in the solution in a cool, dark place until the foliage shows a change in colour. The time the process

takes will vary with the different foliages and, to a certain extent, the temperature in which you are working. It usually takes a few days, but hard woody materials like laurel and rhododendron may take weeks. It is important to take them out when the undersides of the leaves appear slightly oily. Never leave them longer because once this occurs the surface will be slightly sticky and·pick up dust very quickly. The stems can now be stored in a large container in a cool, dry, airy place.

Some leaves can be totally immersed but you need a shallow bath in which to float the individual leaves. As soon as they start to change colour, lift them from the solution, and wash and dry them quickly on blotting paper in a warm place.

Many flowers are dried as heads and are then mounted on false stems made of wire or pieces of straw. The wiring of the flowers may be done before drying because a dry stem is often difficult to wire.

Arranging dried materials calls for exactly the same approach as any other flower arrangement, except that one difficulty is resolved; namely, there is no worry about getting a difficult stem to reach the water! All stems should flow nicely from a central point in the container. Shape, balance and proportion are still important but, because of their visual lightness, dried flowers may often be arranged with slightly taller stems than when using fresh flowers and still look correct. The tracery of lime branches, for example, looks wrong if cut down to use in a low dried arrangement.

Choose your materials as you would fresh flowers, to suit the décor of the room, and try to introduce shades that match a colour already predominant. The container is important, and wood or basket work suit dried materials. Metal is also useful, particularly brass and copper for green, brown and bronze colourings. Pewter looks good with mauve-pink and silver-green shades. China and pottery also offer plenty of scope but should normally be in the rather heavy designs rather than delicately shaped fine china. Silver and cut glass are not in keeping with dried materials.

Ordinary wire netting will be perfectly satisfactory to use to hold the stems in position but because many dried stems will be much thinner, having shrunk during drying out, you may find a closer tangle of netting will help you. Let the netting lie along the base of the vase to steady any stems which may move about.

Dry Oasis and Styrofoam (this can only be used dry) are excellent for holding dry materials, but in both cases they must be firmly held in the container before commencing the arrangement. There is a special Oasis pinholder which can be fixed to the base of the Oasis block to weight it when dry. Ordinary pinholders are not much use with dried materials. I like to use a little wire netting with the Oasis because I find it helps to hold the stems more firmly, and a piece of netting can be bent to hold a difficult stem. Dry sand and fine gravel can be used as a last resort; they have the advantage of being heavy, but they tend to be rather messy and it is difficult to get some of the fine stems into them.

ABOVE This unusual dried arrangement is done in a block of Oasis standing in a wooden cigar box. In the centre are lotus seed heads. The small reed mace, sprayed with hair lacquer to preserve it, sets the height, and the outline foliage is glycerined beech. The large single leaves at the centre are from *Magnolia grandiflora*. Other materials are eucalyptus seed pods, black water grass, wheat, iris seed pods, *Physalis franchetii* and *Helichrysum*. Some of the materials have been dyed or made up artificially.

LEFT:

This is an idea to follow when space is very restricted. It should be used for a special occasion or, as in this picture, for the Winter period using dried flowers. A batten of 1 in wood has been covered with a 1½ in wide velvet ribbon and on to this have been fixed two posies of dried flowers. The bottom one is slightly larger. They are made up of *Statice*, small *Helichrysum*, *Gnaphalium* and flowers from South Africa in the right colours. The whole bunch is held in position with a posy frill.

They could be used all round the room for a party and at the end given to each lady as she leaves.

The ribbon covered battens can be finished with a bow at the top and each posy should have shaded ribbons of different widths to hold the frill in position. The colour scheme should be co-ordinated to the room.

In this picture we also have a flower tree to match. Made on a ribbon covered stick set in a base of cement in a small flower pot covered in moss, the whole arrangement is placed in a china pot holder.

Flower trees have been made in one form or another for many years and they always seem popular and never fail to cause comment.

The ribbon covered stem holds a ball of moss or oasis into which are stuck the stems of dried flowers. In this picture you can see a base of moss and *Hydrangea* with *Statice*, *Helichrysum* and *Gnaphalium* flowers used to form the tree. A few bows and tapered ribbon ends complete off the tree.

RIGHT:

Light from the window to the left of this picture highlights the preserved Beech and Box in this dried collection. The flowers are Achillea, Statice, bronze-yellow Helichrysum, (some have had to be wired on artificial stems) and seed heads and grasses from South Africa. This is an ideal mixture for placing against a wall covering of this texture.

RIGHT:

Dried flowers and foliages fill this old pewter mug. The container, being heavy, needs no extra weight added to make it stand well. The two foliages are glycerined beech and dried *Eucalyptus*.

ABOVE:

A dried arrangement consisting of 3 reed mace (small bullrush), branches of beech with nuts still attached to the twigs and also one or two sprays made up on wires. Oats, *Nigella* and poppy seed heads, a stem of green *Amaranthus* and short larch twigs with cones, *Eucalyptus* flower pods and a few small flower heads from South Africa. The dark foliage giving 'weight' to the arrangement are preserved *Magnolia grandiflora* leaves which have been mounted on wire stems. All have been arranged in a modern six-sided cylinder vase and the stems are held firmly in Oasis 'Sec'.

RIGHT:

This antique dome is very Victorian and may not be to everybody's taste. It was given to me many years ago by a group of people working in our artificial flower workshop and each item was made by a different person. All the stems have been bound together to make a collection rather than an arrangement. No-one could imagine that the contents are all made from crêpe paper. Each flower, leaf or fruit has been modelled from a real item. The flower petals have been carefully cut to shape and hand painted, then wired up and treated.

Materials for drying

Acanthus mollis (Bear's Breeches)
The flowers of this plant can be used in both fresh and dried groups and are interesting in shape and colour. They dry very easily when hung upside down in a dark airy position, or they can be placed in large polythene bags with silica gel for quick drying.

Achillea
These flat heads of yellow flowers are well worth growing for cutting fresh and they dry well. Remove all leaves before treating the stems. They can be hung upside down or laid in flat boxes and dusted in borax. Keep well sealed until fully dried.

Acroclinium (sometimes known as Helipterum)
These are fairly small daisy-type flowers and come in pink and white colourings. They are useful in both the fresh and dried form.

Allium
All the onion family are worth drying and range from quite small seed heads to those of considerable size. They dry readily when hung in airy conditions. One disadvantage is that they tend to retain a slight onion smell.

Amaranthus caudatus (Love-lies-bleeding)
This is an excellent plant with long red tassels, and its green form, A. caudatus 'Viridis', is sold fresh in some flower shops. It should have its leaves removed and be hung upside down to allow the long tassels to dry. It will fade a little but is very useful in tall dried groups and looks well arranged against a background of a darker foliage.

Atriplex hortensis rubra
This has dark red leaves and a flower head closely resembling spinach. Remove all leaves and hang it upside down. When dried, it has interesting arched branches of pendant seeds. It can be a nuisance in the garden because it readily seeds everywhere.

Helichrysum (Straw Flower)
This is a double daisy flower in shades of white, ivory, lemon, pink, maroon, gold and brown. It is grown from seed each year and requires a well-drained and sunny situation to develop well. The stems need careful staking and support to remain straight. They should be cut when fully developed, have the basal leaves removed, be tied in bunches, and hung upside down to dry in an airy, shaded place. For perfect flowers, pick each one just as it starts to open and dry it in a box containing a drying agent, such as silica gel.

Hydrangea
Some varieties are much better than others for drying. The colours range from white, green, deep pink and red to pale and deep blue. The flowers must be cut when they have lost their first softness and are becoming slightly papery and crisp to the touch. They can be dried hung upside down in an airy place or placed in a vase of water, allowing the water to be absorbed gradually, or in a solution of glycerine and water.

Limonium latifolium (Sea Lavender)
Sometimes called perennial statice. It is not unlike gypsophila in habit and has a tiny blue flower which dries well. It is best dried standing upright in a plastic bucket, away from bright light, allowing plenty of air and space between the stems.

Lunaria biennis (Honesty)
Although normally grown for the silvery, moon-shaped membranes between the seed pods, the whole seed pods of this plant can be used, and their grey-green colour suits some arrangements better than the natural silver of the central membrane. The stems must be dried as soon as they are fully developed; if left too long the seed stains the silver membranes. When the outer seed cases are dry they will easily peel off. They are now sold dyed in many colours but are better used in their natural colour.

Molucella laevis (Bells of Ireland)
This does well in some seasons but is not always successful. It is now often sold as a cut flower, imported from Kenya and South America in its green form. The tall slender square stems look well in large arrangements and it has beautiful papery green cup-shaped calyxes. It takes glycerine well and can also be bleached by drying in heated conditions. All foliage should be removed carefully before drying.

Physalis (Chinese Lantern)
The interest in this member of the potato family lies not in its flowers but in the pretty orange/scarlet seed heads which remain at the end of the season and hang like lanterns down the stem. One form, P. edulis, is grown for its edible fruit. Dry it by hanging it up, having first bunched it into a small number of stems. Remove the leaves as they dry and, when the lanterns are completely dry, lay in a box with a little silica gel.

Statice sinuata
This is sold in August and September as a fresh flower and dried for use in the Winter months. It comes in white, yellow, mauve and pink, and is often available as a mixed bunch. It is very long lasting and needs

thinning carefully to get a good shape before arranging. Another statice which can be dried is *S. suworowii* and this has long square stems of lilac pink flower sprays.

Ferns and bracken are best dried between newspaper just as they are taking up colour in the autumn. Leave them under a carpet to keep them flat and they should dry well in a few weeks. Ornamental grasses have many shapes and sizes and are useful either on their own or arranged with mixed flowers. There are many other plants that can be dried and you should experiment with other annuals and materials from the flower border. Seed heads are very useful and should be cut from the plant when nearly dry but not weathered. A walk along a country lane can provide many more items, but protected plants must not be gathered (see page 14).

BELOW All the materials in this cupid vase come from the garden and have been dried naturally, with the exception of the box (*Buxus*) which has been bleached and glycerined.

Artificial (silk) flowers

Artificial materials are not new – they have been made in some form for many years. They have always had a use and always will be used. If not liked (many people say they could not live with them), this may be because they have not been well arranged. They are ideal for a dark area where nothing else will grow.

They can be of two distinct kinds; either a copy of something true to life, and many of these are very good today, or something very way-out which I would prefer to call 'fun flowers' – these are more for exhibition display work rather than of use in home decorating. I do not believe you can mix the two.

There is a very wide range in the price of so called 'silk flowers' and you only get what you pay for so to speak. Some of the so called 'silk' or 'polyester silk' are not able to be washed because for cheapness fabric leaves are added. Another point to watch is that the flower dyes do not run. For long lasting qualities one must go for the very best – it pays every time.

Arrange in exactly the same way as if you were working with fresh materials. I like to use the oasis 'Sec' as a media for holding the 'stems' but ordinary dry moss can be secured into the vase with a layer of wire netting over the top (clip the netting firmly over the vase rim). It is important to have a firm base and a layer of dry sand or gravel to help with the balance if using a light container.

I believe the secret in keeping these arrangements looking good is (1) to be seasonal and (2) not to allow them to become dusty or dirty. Keep shaking or blowing them and wash from time to time by dipping in warm mild soapy water and drying them immediately by hanging upside down in a warm airy place.

If you wish to use 'silk' mixed with fresh flowers, varnish the stems to waterproof them and then they will not rust.

LEFT:
Mixed *narcissi* (Polyantha type) in an old wooden cheese press – simply arranged with a piece of rock and stones to cover the soil. A little moss adds more colour.

PAGES 142–3
A table centre in mixed cream and yellow flowers and foliages including variegated ivy and golden tradescantia, maidenhair fern and leather fern. The main flowers are yellow spray carnations, roses and *Alstroemeria*.

ABOVE:
A Tazza shaped vase chosen years ago by Constance Spry for a country potter to make and one which has proved most successful. Its wide open centre allows great freedom to the arranger to thread stems at all angles to the centre of the vase.

Mixed greens have been chosen for this arrangement and include ivies, maidenhair fern, *Eucalyptus*, *Tradescantia*, Ladder fern, *Peperomia* and *Chlorophytum*.

A bronze Warwick vase is used for this arrangement after the Dutch School. Silk flowers are ideal for a composition of this type because they can be purchased singly.

The group includes a flag Iris, paeony, *Hydrangea*, *Clematis*, lilac, *Freesia*, poppy, a *Gladioli*, hyacinth, *Agapanthus*, *Narcissi*, Guelder rose, *Rhododendron* and *Alstroemeria*.

In groups of this kind, the flowers are placed closer together in the base to give weight to the vase and little foliage is used. The range of materials used takes in many months of flowering – early Spring for the *Narcissi* up to *Agapanthus* in the Autumn.

Often the colourings are muted so care must be taken when choosing your materials.

Fruits and foliages from the hedgerow with small poppies, daisies and also cornflowers to add colour. They are arranged in a small coloured glass container.

The height is obtained from the stem of dock and the outline flowers are the sprays of blackberry and wild clematis. The centre is a cluster of wild strawberries in fruit and flower. These are not all made from washable materials – only the flower petals are silk – the foliages, fruits and stems are fabric which cannot be washed.

Plants in decoration

Flowering and foliage plants have for very many years been used in house decoration. In early times they were used to fill fireplaces and also they seemed to fill all the windowsills, growing in their clay pots which stood on saucers to stop the water from draining out and marking the woodwork.

Today, there is a tendency to group them more together to make a decoration or have individual specimen plants standing in a decorative pot holder within the room.

When using plants in a group one considers exactly the same principles as when arranging flowers; colours, shape of leaf, upright growth for the back and something trailing over the side even to the large leafed or bold flowering plants for the 'focal point' at the centre.

Different growing requirements (one may need a lot of moisture and another to be rather dry) can be a problem. However, one can have all the plants kept as individuals in their separate pots by standing them together on a tin lined tray or shallow dish.

Keep the base of the container with a layer of gravel or damp sand. This will give a moist growing atmosphere around the plant when they are growing in a dry atmosphere.

Fill in between pots with lichen moss, bun moss, bark and stone.

If, when using a group of mixed foliage plants, one wants to make these more interesting for a special occasion, hide a couple of test tubes or flower cones between the pots and into these place the flowering stem, e.g. a couple of Singapore orchids or tuberose. These of course can be in water so will last well. While they may not make much show on their own, they will become important in this group.

With this method of displaying pot plants one can change the plants easily. A semi permanent foliage background can have flowering plants popped in for the flowering period. A pot of daffodils or hyacinths can be added without disturbing any roots when they are at an interesting stage and removed straight after flowering ready for tulips or a Cineraria to follow.

If this does not appeal, try keeping the growing plants in their own pots dropping them into a deeper container filled with damp peat. This stops the pots drying out so readily and again gives a better growing atmosphere for the plants. Treat each plant as an individual, watering and feeding it when necessary.

A wooden tub is ideal for this but it should have a lining made for it because the soil soon causes the wood to rot away. A metal (preferably zinc lining with handles) will hold the wooden spars firmly in position. I have found to my horror that as the wood dries the sections shrink and the container will collapse.

Growing plants on a plate can be very attractive especially in the early Spring but one must have a fairly deep plate. The old meat dishes with a well for fat were ideal but are very hard to find these days. A plastic seed tray (without drainage holes) or a cat litter tray are excellent because they often have little raised edges at the corners lifting the flat base off the ground (which prevents condensation marking polished furniture).

The secret to success with these is to not fill the container with too many plants. Allow each one to be seen with soil, bark, bun moss, lichen and gravel around them. A large piece of stone, or rock, will add interest. As no drainage is available, however, one must not over water, just keep the soil surface moist.

Have a well balanced open compost and start with it in good condition. This will contain loam, peat to act as a sponge and retain moisture, and coarse sand to keep the compost open for air and good root development. This should not be too wet or too dry – a good test is to squeeze the compost in the hand. It should just retain its moulded shape – neither sticky or crumbly.

Always choose healthy growing plants with a good ball of roots and see that they have been well watered before planting up. You can shape the ball of soil and roots carefully to fit into the container but do not damage them.

One or two large pieces of stone will help hold the plants in position. A small area of gravel will be ideal when watering because moss and soil tend to dry on the top and the water, if one is not careful, will run straight off the surface. Spraying with a fine mist of water will be helpful and keeps the leaf surface clean.

PAGES 148–9

This rather large and colourful rectangular copper pan has been planted up with both flowering and foliage plants. When combining both, the long term foliages will continue to grow and all that one has to do is to replace those that have finished flowering. The *Cyclamen* and *Solanum* for example may be replaced by *Hyacinths* and daffodils. The foliage plants include a *Hedera*, a parlour palm, a *Nephrolepis*, *Tradescantia*, *pilea cadierei* and a *Chlorophytum*. To add extra interest, Lichen covered twigs add a little height and cork bark, moss and gravel cover the soil.

RIGHT:

A beautiful antique Sèvres apple green and gilt urn simply arranged with a few stems of white and cream flowers. The delicate *Symphoricarpus orbicularis* foliage is a special feature because it was picked from a Kent garden in mid November.

A Sterling Star lily, 3 stems of Singapore orchids and a few white *Freesia* complete the simple flowing lines to this arrangement.

LEFT:
A shallow round dish of Cacti and succulents makes a change from the more usual planted dish. The placing of the plants to get the maximum value from leaf shapes and colours is very important and the use of heavy pieces of rock, gravel and sand give the whole collection a more dramatic appearance. In this arrangement the most important plant (from the decorative angle) is *Agave Americana variegata* which has been planted slightly on its side so that the shape and colouring shows up well. These plants need careful and restricted watering, as there is no free drainage, and plenty of natural light.

ABOVE:
This antique wooden tub is a great favourite of mine. To keep it in good order, I have had a zinc lining made and now keep it filled with mixed foliage plants. Its depth allows fairly substantial plants to grow happily and in this picture you can see *Ficus elastica decora, Hedera canariensis variegata, Sansevieria trifasciata,* the small leaved *Hedera* 'Eva', *Dieffenbachia* 'Camilla', *Tradescantia, Heptapleurum arboricolum* and variegated Buffalo grass.

Plants suitable for growing as a mixed overall arrangement or in foliage groups.

Flowering	**Just Foliage**
Anthurium	Aralia
Azalea	Aspidistra elatior
Begonia	Begonia rex
Cineraria	Chlorophytum
Cyclamen	elatum
Gloxinia	Cissus antarctica
Hydrangea	Cyperus
Kalenchoe	alternifolius
Poinsettia	Euonymus
Primula	Fatshedera lizei
malacoides	Hedera (ivies)
obconica	Maranta
sinensis	Peperomia
Saintpaulia	Pilea cadierei
Solanum	Rhoicissus
Schizanthus	rhomboidea
	Sansevieria
Bulbs for short	Saxifraga
period displays	sarmentosa
	Scindapsus
Cacti	Syngonium
	podophyllum
	Tradescantia
	Ferns

This is a copy of an idea that Constance Spry thought up many years ago. It is a collection of plants, all left in their individual pots so that they can all receive their own special treatment so that water-loving plants and also those needing drier conditions can be grouped together. They are placed on a tin-lined shallow basketware tray. Damp gravel in the base will allow a moist atmosphere around the plants. Some are stood up on tripods at different levels to give a variation in height.

To add extra interest, two flower cones (tubes) holding water have been hidden in the foliage and the stems of Sterling Star lilies are arranged in these. This allows more colour to be brought in for special occasions, and the odd flower, of little use on its own, may well be displayed in a group.

The high gloss to the grape ivy (*Rhoicissus rhomboidea*) in the centre of this photograph comes from the light reflecting off leaves recently sprayed with leaf shine.

Plans included in this group are *Hedera canariensis variegata*, *Dracaena terminalis*, *Dieffenbachia*, *Chamaedorea elegans*, *Philodendron scandens*, *Scindapsus aureus*, *Chlorophytum variegatum* and *Peperomia magnoliaefolia*.

OVERLEAF: A table centre in mixed flowers and foliages including variegated ivy and golden tradescantia, maidenhair fern and leather fern.

A-Z

A

Abutilon
P. Summer.
This plant is grown essentially for its foliage, but the small flowers can be used. Flowers: bell shape, orange with red veins, not long lasting. Foliage: variegated due to a virus. A. *megapotamicum* E.S. (greenhouse): flowers have red caps with yellow petals on small graceful arching sprays.
● Hot water for both foliage stems and flower sprays.

Acacia
Mimosa. E.T. and S.
* From February.
Flowers: yellow, very short lived in their fluffy state. Foliage: A. *dealbata* has many leaflets forming compound leaves giving it a fluffy appearance; A. *longifolia* has a long linear leaf.
● Use on its own, not mixed with other flowers. Keep sealed up in the cool until needed. It is best in a moist atmosphere.

Acanthus mollis
Bear's Breeches. P. Summer.
Flowers: white and purple, tubular on long spikes; dry well. Foliage: thistle-like.
● Young material will not last long so foliage must be fully developed before it is cut and then given a long drink before arranging. Flower stems are hollow and may benefit from filling with water and plugging.

Acer
Maple. D.T. and S. * common form only. May-Autumn.
The common field maple is lovely when just opening in Spring. Japanese maples are very decorative small shrubs. Maples have lovely Autumn colourings and attractive bark.
● Hammer woody stems and soak for a few hours in water. Revive when necessary by placing tips in boiling water. Some of the fine-leaved varieties may have difficulty taking up water.

Achillea

Achillea
Yarrow. P. * Early Summer–Autumn.
A. *filipendulina*: flowers are various shades of yellow, sometimes sold dried. A. *millefolium* 'Cerise Queen': flowers are pink, long lasting, and strong smelling. A. *ptarmica* 'The Pearl': flowers are white and their round pompom shape is quite different from other yarrows.
● Remove lower foliage as it smells in water. Dry by hanging upside down or lay the flower heads dusted in borax in a box.

Acidanthera
Corm. *
September–November.
Flowers: white with purple spot at base of flower; fragrant and long lasting.
● As for gladioli.

Aconitum
Monkshood. P. Summer.
Flowers: purple-coloured flower spike, useful for mixed Summer arrangements; lasts well. Similar to some delphiniums but has a much smaller flower spike. The roots of this plant are poisonous. Dry the seed head by hanging upside down.

Adiantum
Maidenhair Fern. P.
* cut and treat as a pot plant most of the year. Foliage: useful for bouquets and it goes particularly well with sweet peas in arrangements. Most attractive when arranged on its own giving a cool effect.
● Burn cut tips to seal stem. Float in a bath of water for a good drink.

Agapanthus

Agapanthus
African Lily. P.
* July-September.
Flowers: blue or white on long leafless stems, useful for large groups but not long lasting. The many small flowers which make up the round heads are wired singly by florists in bouquets. Seed-bearing heads can be dried for Autumn.
● A long drink is necessary before they are arranged.

Agrostemma
syn. *Lychnis* (q.v.)

Alchemilla mollis

Alchemilla mollis
Lady's Mantle. P.
* June-August.
One of the most useful plants, this mixes well with many flowers. Flowers: sharp green colour.
● Remove basal leaves and give a good drink before arranging.

Allium
Lily family, related to onions. Bulb.
* May-August.
Flowers: yellow (A. *moly*), white (A. *triquetrum*), red and green (A. *siculum*), bright lilac (A. *giganteum*); sizes vary; many good as dried seed heads.

Alnus
Alder. D.T.
* February and March.
Use when in flower or leaf; branches are elegantly shaped and carry catkins and cones at the same time. The catkins make a lot of pollen dust when fully out.
● Cut alder in December and bring it into the warm to force it.

Alstroemeria
Peruvian Lily. P.
* Nearly all year round
from glasshouse crops,
outdoor flowering
June-August.
Flowers: cream and yellow,
red, pink and mauve,
orange and yellow, white,
brown; long slender stems;
last well in water. Foliage:
rather untidy and is easily
damaged when packed for
market. Stems are easily
cut down to be used in
small arrangements. It is a
very useful plant.
● Remove basal leaves and
stand in deep water for a
few hours to really charge
the stems with moisture.

Alstroemeria

Althaea rosea
Hollyhock, P. July.
Flowers: pastel cream,
pink, white or yellow; old
fashioned double and
single form. Suitable for a
large group or a Dutch
group; last well.
● Hollow stems.

Amaranthus caudatus
Love-lies-bleeding. A.
* August–October.
Flowers: green or red, can
be dried; best in tall groups
where hanging panicle can
show to good advantage.
● Remove most of the
leaves before placing in
deep water. Stems may be
woody some seasons and
need splitting.

Amaryllis belladonna
Belladonna Lily. Bulb.
* August–October.
Flowers: pink flower spike;
long lasting; leafless stem.

● Cut stems at an angle
and allow a long drink.

Amelanchier
D.S. Spring and Autumn.
White-flowered shrub in
April. Good Autumn
colour.
● Remove some of the
foliage to allow full benefit
from flowers. Woody stem.

Anchusa
P. Sumer.
Flowers: blue, stems like
large forget-me-nots up to
1 metre (3 feet) tall; long
lasting.
● Remove many of the
basal leaves. This plant
wilts easily.

**Andromeda
floribunda**
syn. *Pieris floribunda (q.v.)*

Anemone
Tuber. * October–June.
Flowers: colourful and long
lasting. Double and single
forms, some named
varieties such as 'The
Bride' (white) and
'September Charm' are
good. Give a long drink up
to their necks in water
before arranging. Does not
last well in Oasis.

Anemone pulsatilla
syn. *Pulsatilla vulgaris*
(q.v.)

Anemone

Angelica
P. * June onwards.
Useful for seed heads in
late Summer but not long
lasting as flowers. Up to 2
metres (6 feet) tall.
● Put in water straight
after cutting, place a cane

in hollow stem and plug.

Anthemis
P. July–August.
Flowers: yellow daisy, long
lasting. Foliage: aromatic,
fernlike.

Anthurium
Flamingo Flower. P.
* All year round glasshouse
flower. Flowers: white,
cream, coral or scarlet.
Useful for modern
arrangements and last
well.
● Warm water if limp.

Antirrhinum
Snapdragon. A.
* March–June, late
Autumn.
Flowers: long single flower
stems, red, pink, white,
orange, yellow; long
lasting, useful for big
arrangements. Some very
good hybrid forms.
● Give a deep long drink
before arranging and
remove much of the lower
foliage. The early crops
from glasshouses have
rather fragile stems.

Aquilegia
Columbine. P. * Early
Summer.
Flowers: cottage garden
type: pretty pastel shades
which arrange well in
pewter, copper and silver;
last well, buds keep
opening. Foliage:
attractive Autumn colours.

Aquilegia

Aralia elata
E.S. Autumn–Winter.
Foliage: individual
ivy-type leaves, good for
centre of flower group.

● Place leaf tips in boiling
water then immerse stems
in cold water for a good long
drink.

Arbutus
Strawberry Tree. E.T.
* Sometimes
October–December.
Flowers: strawberry-like
fruits at the same time as
small white bell-shaped
flowers (October–
December); unusual in
arrangements. Foliage:
thin out leaves to let fruits
show up well.

Arctotis
A. Later Summer.
Flowers: daisy flowers,
close up at night; many
hybrid colour forms, quite
long lasting.

Arisarum proboscideum
Mouse Plant. P.
March–May.
Flowers: mouse-like in
appearance–stalk 7–15 cm
(3–6 inches) long, spathe
greyish white and inflated
with long curved tail up to
12 cm (5 inches);
interesting flower for
children. Foliage: small
arum-shaped leaves.

Armeria
Thrift. P. June–August.
Flowers: white, pink or
lilac; useful in small
arrangements.

Artemisia
A. abrotanum
(Southernwood), *A.
absinthium* (Wormwood).
P. Late Spring–Summer.
Foliage: aromatic
silver-grey.
● Place tips in boiling
water, then give a long
drink before arranging.

Arum italicum pictum
P. Autumn, Winter and
Spring.
Foliage: beautifully veined
and arrow-shaped in
varying sizes: red berries
last well and appear in late
summer.
● Soak before use.

Arundinaria
Bamboo. O. * dried.
All year round.
Best used as a dry material, does not take water well.
● Press under carpet to keep from curling.

Asparagus
P. * (outdoor and greenhouse grown).
All year round.
A. officinalis: July and August.
After taking the edible tops of young sprouts, cut as foliage. *A. plumosus* (Asparagus Fern): formerly used in large quantities as the background to flowers in wedding bouquets. *A. sprengeri*: often grown in hanging baskets, can be cut but watch for spiteful thorns. *A. asparagoides* (Smilax): available most of the year, used for garlanding.

Aspidistra
Houseplant. * All year.
Foliage: dark green and variegated forms; use as single leaves in mixed greens; bleached leaves are used with dried materials.
● Submerge in water to get a good drink before arranging.

Asplenium
P. Fern. * *A. bulbiferum*.
All year round.
This is the fern that produces little plantlets on the fronds which root readily. Cut and use the fronds with mixed greens.
● Submerge in water for a long drink.

Aster

Aster
Michaelmas Daisy. P.
* July–October.
Flowers: daisy-type; blue, white, pink or red; many are subject to mildew and wilt; useful for large mixed autumn groups.
● Stems of some are woody so hammer well before giving a long drink.

Astilbe
False Goat's Beard. P.
* June–August as a pot plant.
Flowers: pink and white colours.
● Hammer stems and place tips in hot water. Foliage curls up very quickly if it becomes at all dry.

Astrantia

Astrantia
P. June and July.
Flowers: artificial looking, silvery pink-green with deeper pink centre.
Foliage: does not last well in water if left on long stems. Variegated foliage form of *A. minor* is excellent.
● Plung into water straight after cutting. Dry by hanging upside down.

Atriplex
Orach, a form of spinach. A.
July–August.
Flowers: crimson colouring. Seeds very readily; can be dried.
● Remove basal leaves and give a long drink; stems may be woody so hammer well if necessary.

Aucuba
Spotted Laurel. E.S.

March–April (berries), April–May (flowers).
* as a growing plant.
Foliage: useful for mixed greens or centre of a large group; lasts well.

Auricula
P. April–July.
Flowers: old-fashioned type, allied to polyanthus; useful for small arrangements; longer lasting than polyanthus.
Foliage cannot be used.

Azalea
E. and D.S. (Correctly known as Rhododendron). *
Cut stems April–June and late Autumn and Winter as pot plants.
Flowers: superb range of colours, shape and size; show off well in copper and pewter containers, long lasting.
● Woody stems. Pot plants must always be kept moist.

Begonia
P. * as a pot plant.
Most of the year.
A very large group of plants–can be divided into flowering and foliage plants. The 'Rex' group are the main foliage ones. Some of the species are very pretty and last well when cut. The large-flowered varieties do not last when cut.
● Submerge foliage before use.

Berberis
Barberry. E. and D.S.
* Late Winter–June.

Flowers and berries are useful.
Foliage: attractive Autumn colour and a variety of leaf shapes. Best varieties are *B. darwinii*, *B. gagnepainii*, *B. thunbergii atropurpurea*, *B. wilsonae*.
● Put in hot water after hammering stems. Spines can be poisonous.

Bergenia
syn. *Megasea*, Giant Saxifrage, Elephant's Ears.
All year round (foliage), Spring and Summer (flowers).
Flowers: *B. cordifolia* are pink in March, *B. crassifolia* are deep red in May, June. Foliage: flat leathery rounded leaves in a variety of shapes and colours. Only use mature leaves.
● Float leaves before use if soft to allow them to absorb plenty of moisture.

Betula
Birch. T. Spring and Summer.
Branches: light tracery, some catkins in early Spring. Silver grey bole.
● Hammer base of stem.

Bocconia
syn. *Macleaya* (q.v.)

Briza gracilis
Quaking Grass. A.
* sometimes. Late Summer.
To dry: hang up young grass in Autumn in small bunches in an airy room.

Brodiaea uniflora
Bulb. * April–May.
Flowers: pale lilac and star-shaped on leafless stems; long lasting.

Buddleia
Semi-E.S. May–August.
B. davidii (July–August) is common; *B. globosa* (May–June) is unusual with bright yellow fragrant flower balls.
● Remove most of the

foliage and hammer the stems.

Buxus
Box. E.S. * common form only. Nearly all year.
Foliage: variegated small-leaved varieties with white edge to leaf are the most interesting; long lasting and good for mixed greens. *B. sempervirens argentea* or *B. aurea maculata* are recommended.
● Hammer woody stems.

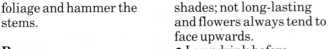

Caladium
Houseplant. * All year round.
Foliage: large arrow-shaped leaves—reds, pinks, cream and greens; place the whole pot plant in the centre of a large arrangement.
● Will not stand draughts or cold conditions.

Calendula officinalis

Calendula
Pot Marigold. A.
* March–October.
July–October in the garden.
Flowers: colourful, particularly the cream and yellow and pale orange

shades; not long-lasting and flowers always tend to face upwards.
● Long drink before arranging.

Calla aethiopica
syn. *Zantedeschia aethiopica (q.v.)*

Callistemon
Bottle Brush, E.S.
June–August.
Flowers: red, resemble a bottle brush.
● Hard woody stems. Best to cut into the wood just below the flower and not the really old wood.

Callistephus
China Aster. A.
* August–October.
Flowers: various forms from small buttons to large shaggy flowers; pink, red, mauve, blue and white; last well.
● Remove all foliage from base of stem to stop unpleasant smell in water; some stems may be quite woody.

Callistephus

Calluna vulgaris
syn *Erica vulgaris* (q.v.)

Camellia japonica
E.S. * Foliage mainly in Autumn and Winter.
Flowers in Spring.
Flowers: on short stems and very fragile. Foliage: often shows yellowing on leaves which is very attractive.
● Woody stems; never cut when young growth is soft.

Campanula
Bellflower. A.B. and P.

* July and August.
Flowers: long lasting bell shapes in blue, mauve, white and pink; some stems may be woody. *C. medium* 'Calycanthema' (Canterbury Bell) is the old fashioned cup and saucer variety. It is a biennial. *C. persicifolia* is the usual market variety. It is a perennial.

Canna
Indian Shot Plant. P.
Summer.
Flowers: red and yellow, not always successful in England. Foliage: some red-coloured, good for large groups, rather similar to Dieffenbachia in habit but self-coloured and variegated.
● Place in deep water straight after cutting.

Carpinus betulus
Hornbeam. D.T.
Spring and Summer.
Foliage: good-shaped branches for backing a large group; takes glycerine well for Winter use.
● Hammer stems.

Caryopteris clandonensis
D.S. August–September.
Flowers: blue; last quite well.

Cassinia fulvida
E.S. All year round (foliage) July (flowers).
Foliage: rather like Veronica; yellow-green, variety of shapes; lasts well. Flowers: small white heads.

Catananche
Cupid's Dart. A.P.
* Summer.
Flowers: blue and white, look rather artificial; useful for mixed small arrangements; good for drying.

Ceanothus
E. and D.S. May–July.
Flowers: blues, last well in

water. *C.* 'Gloire de Versailles' is a good variety.
● Woody stems.

Centaurea

Centaurea
Cornflower. A.B. and P. *
A. only Summer.
Flowers: perennial form has blue or white flowers, annual form has deep and pale blues, white and wine-red flowers. Foliage: silver-green. *C. montana* is a good perennial form. *C. moschata* (Sweet Sultan) is an annual with white, yellow and purple flowers.

Centranthus
see *Kentranthus*.

Cephalaria tatarica
syn. *Scabiosa elata* (q.v.)

Chaenomeles lagenaria
Quince, Japonica. D.S.
Early Spring.
Flowers: red, pink and white; blossom in clusters just when foliage breaks; fruits in Autumn.
● Remove leaves from base of stem.

Cheiranthus
Wallflower. P. (treated as B.) * April and May.
Flowers: sweet-smelling yellow, red, bronze. Not long lasting.
● Hammer stems and remove foliage from near water or it will smell.

Chimonanthus fragrans
Wintersweet. D.S.
November–March.
Flowers: pale yellow on leafless branches; fragrant; ideal for specimen vase.

161

Useful Winter shrub.
● Very woody stems need splitting.

Chionodoxa luciliae
Bulb. * Sometimes. Early Spring.
Flowers: pretty blue, ideal for moss gardens with snowdrops and primroses.
● Cut stems without any trace of white at base.

Choisya ternata
Mexican Orange Blossom. E.S.
* Autumn and Spring.
Foliage: useful all year round. Flowers: fragrant white.

Chrysanthemum
A. and P. * All year round.
Flowers: single and double compound heads or single blooms; many colours and varieties. Very long lasting and useful. Some people prefer them as an Autumn/Winter flower.
● Hammer stems and give a long drink.

Chrysanthemum

Cineraria maritima
syn. *Senecio cineraria* P. Spring and Summer.
Foliage: silver-grey, good for small arrangements. Flowers: very insignificant.
● Stems sometimes do not take up water, use young shoots only and hammer well.

Clarkia
A. * Summer.
Flowers: single or double form in mauves, pinks, whites; very useful for cutting. *C. elegans* is the

one most commonly grown.
● Soft stem treatment, and remove unnecessary foliage.

Clematis
P. Spring and Summer.
Flowers: not long lasting in water but can be very striking in large groups or as a table centre. *C. armandii*: white, April and May; *C. cirrhosa*: cream, January and March; *C. montana*: white and pink, May and June; *C. jackmanii*: large-flowered, mauve, pink, purple, July–October.
● Boiling water for flower stems.

Clematis

Clivia
Bulb. * Sprin and Summer.
Flowers: reddish-yellow colour; some cream forms in seedlings. Foliage: evergreen. Often sold in shops as one leaf and one flower stem together.

Cobaea
Cup and Saucer Plant. A. * Pot plants May–June, garden flowers July–October. Requires sun and a wall to grow up.
Flowers: t rumpet-shaped in violet and cream and green. Can be used when the tubular corolla has dropped aænd the calyx remains attached to the stem.
● Cut short flower stems and place in water straight away.

Colchicum
Erroneously known as Autumn Crocus. Bulb. Autumn.

Flowers: pinkish particularly pretty in double form; not long lasting.
● Put in water straight after cutting.

Coleus
Nettle family. P.
* May–June.
Foliage: very decorative, loses brilliant colouring in Winter.
● Foliage very soft and must go into water immediately after cutting. Single leaves do not last – the whole shoot must be used.

Colutea arborescens
Bladder Senna. D.S. Late Summer.
Flowers: yellow-brown pea shaped followed by bladder-like inflated pods in September:
● Woody stems.

Convallaria majalis

Convallaria majalis
Lily-of-the-Valley. P.
* Forced lily-of-the-valley is available all year round. Garden flowers in May–July.
Flowers: mostly white, pink form is less popular and seldom seen. Foliage: garden valley has very much darker foliage than the forced valley.
● Place stems in water straight after cutting; use warm water if they are limp and it may help to crush the tips.

Coreopsis
P. * Summer.
Flowers: yellow daisy-type, light and delicate; look well

arranged with grasses and seed heads.

Coreopsis

Cornus
Dogwood. D.S. Winter, Early Spring.
C. mas (Cornelian Cherry): early flowering–February, March. *C. alba* and *C. stolonifera* have good red-coloured branches in Winter. Wild Dogwood is also a useful flowering shrub.

Cornus

Cortaderia argentea
Pampas Grass. P.
* Autumn.
Sharp-pointed reed-like foliage. Useful for large groups in Autumn, such as Harvest Festival and for dried arrangements. Cut when young and hang upside down for drying.

Corylopsis pauciflora
D.S. * Spring.
Delicate soft yellow catkins in Spring followed by attractive foliage.
● Woody stem.

RIGHT A mixed green arrangement in a round wicker basket.

Corylus avellana
Hazel. D.T.
Autumn–Spring.
Cobnuts in Autumn;
catkins in Winter and early
Spring. Useful dainty
foliage. *C. avellana*
'Contorta' has attractive
twisted branches.
● Woody stem treatment.

Cosmos bipinnatus
A. * occasionally.
Late Summer.
Flowers: daisy-type, useful
for cutting; mostly pinks,
purples and whites; last
well. Foliage very light and
delicate.

Cotoneaster
D. and E.S. Autumn,
Spring.
Flowers: late Spring, but
more noted for its Autumn
berries—red, scarlet, and
some yellow and black.
Foliage: useful for cutting.

Crataegus
Hawthorn, May. D.S.
Autumn and Spring.
Good for Spring flowers and
Autumn fruiting. Wild
variety has a range of berry
colours. Some people will
not allow it in the house
when in flower.

Crinum
Bulb. * occasionally.
September and October.
Flowers: lily-type; thick
fleshy stems. Grows
untidily. Because of its
heavy flowers it is only
good for large vases.

Crocosmia
Garden Montbretia. Corm.
* August–late Summer.
Superior form of
Montbretia. Flowers:
yellow-brown to orange,
good lasting qualities.
Foliage can be used
without flowers – very
similar to Iris but smaller.

Crocus
Bulb. * as a pot plant. Spring.
Not often used for
arrangements because
flowers last a very short
time when cut; best used in
a planted garden on a plate.

Cucurbita
Gourds. A. Late Summer.
Fruits: decorative and
non-edible; good in mixed
fruit groups; should last
throughout the Winter.
● Harvest just before the
frost and allow to ripen
gently in a dry airy place;
handle with great care as
they can be easily bruised
and will rot; can be
varnished but are better
natural.

Cyclamen
Corm. * as a pot plant.
Autumn and Spring.
Flowers: last well when
picked. Foliage: excellent
in small arrangements and
bouquets, some varieties
have attractive markings.
Never throw a plant away
which has finished
flowering as the leaves can
be used with other flowers.
● Cut the stems once they
have been pulled from the
corm and place them in
warm water.

Cynara scolymus
Artichoke, Cardoon. P. *
sometimes.
Late Spring and Autumn.
Foliage: superb silver-grey
large pinnatifid fleshy
leaves. Flowers:
thistle-like when open, can
be dried in Autumn; very
attractive when in bud and
often used in this stage.
● Place in water straight
after cutting.

Cyperus
Umbrella Plant. Pl. * as a
pot plant, most of the year.
Rush-like grass;
interesting shapes to add to
a special mixed green
arrangement.

Cytisus
Broom. E. and D.S. *
April–July.
C. albus: white. *C.
battandieri*: silver foliage,
bright yellow flowers
May–June. *C. praecox*:
creamy-yellow. *C.
scoparius* (Scots Broom):
many named varieties. Not
easy to use as it quickly
looks untidy. In modern
arrangements some forms
of broom are sold in a dry
bleached form.
● Woody stems, hot water if
soft.

Dahlia
Tuber. * July to first frosts.
Flowers: wide colour range,
the best for cutting are the
small decorative, cacti and
pompom types; dahlias are
easily bruised.
● Burn cut tips in a flame;
hollow stems need filling
with warm water.

Dahlia

Daphne
E. and D.S. Spring.
Very good scent in Spring;
plants die out after a
number of years. Good
varieties are *D. cneorum*
(E.), *D. laureola* (E.), *D.
mezereum* (D.), *D. pontica*
(D.).

Datura suaveolens
Angel's Trumpet. E.S.
(glasshouse) Summer.

D. stramonium (Thorn
Apple) is a weed which has
decorative inflated seed
pods with prickles when
setting seed. Hang up to
dry in a lage polythene bag
to hold the seeds if the pods
burst to stop them
spreading. It is poisonous.

Delphinium
P. * Late Spring/Summer.
Flowers: wide range of
colours–blue, mauve,
purple, cream, white and
pink. By cutting back after
flowering to the first leaves
on its stem, secondary
flower stems will be
produced in late Summer
which will be smaller but
easier to use. *D. ajacis*
(Larkspur): A.
* Summer. Very useful
since a spike-shaped flower
arranges well with round
ones.

Delphinium

Deutzia
D.S. * Summer.
Flowers: white and pink in
June or July in the garden.
Stems are woody.

Dianthus barbatus

Dianthus barbatus
Sweet William. B.
* Late Spring, Summer.
Flowers: old fashioned and

good for cottage-type arrangements; long lasting.

• Hammer stems and remove many of the basal leaves.

Dianthus caryophyllus
Carnation. P. * All year round. Garden flowers in Summer.
Flowers: important commercial flowers and there is a tendency to have dyed ones at the expense of the old fashioned varieties; spray carnations have three or four flowers and buds per stem; border carnations (pinks) are also very useful for arrangements.

Dianthus caryophyllus

Dicentra spectabilis
Bleeding Heart. P. Late Spring–early Summer.
Flowers: arching spray of bell-like flowers in a rosy crimson colour. Foliage: very attractive, lacy in texture, not unlike aquilegia.

Digitalis

Digitalis
Foxglove. B. * occasionally. Summer.

Flowers: useful range of colours and good-shaped flower stem for large groups.

• If stem is hollow, fill with water: remove basal leves and put into water quickly.

Dimorphotheca
A. * May–October.
Flowers: daisy-type; two forms available – *D. barberiae* purple-flowered, *D. ecklonis* white-flowered. Sometimes they close up at night.

Dipsacus sylvestris
Teazle. B. * Late Summer. Ideal for drying for Autumn and Winter arrangements; darker in colour if left on the plant to dry naturally. Found growing wild in some areas.

Dodecatheon
Relative of the primula. P. Early Summer.
Flowers: on a straight stem of 20–30 cm (9–12 inches) rising from a collar of leaves; ideal for a small interesting botanical arrangement rather than a pretty one.

Doronicum
Leopard's Bane. P. * occasionally.
April–May.
Flowers: simple yellow daisies. The first of a new range of flowers after the daffodils, narcissi and hyacinths and its different shape is appreciated at this time of the year.

Echeveria fulgens
P. Late Spring and Summer.
Flowers: unusual on long fleshy stem; long lasting. Foliage: thick and fleshy in a thick rosette; useful as a focal point for a mixed green collection. A very good blue-grey colour and it goes well with apricot shades.

• Hammer base of stem if thick.

Echinops ritro
Globe Thistle. P. July–August.
Flowers: round blue flowers on stems of up to 1 metre (3 feet). A white form is also available. Long lasting, can be dried for winter use.
Foliage: silver grey-green and thistle-like. Very easy to grow.

• Woody stems.

Echinops

Elaeagnus
E. and D.S. All year round. Foliage: often silvery on underside of leaf; lasts well in water; *E. pungens aurea* and *E variegata* have yellow margins to leaves and are excellent in mixed foliage groups. A very worthwhile foliage to grow.

Embothrium
E.T. May–June and Autumn.
Flowers: good red colouring in early Summer and Autumn.

Enkianthus campanulatus
D.S. May.

Flowers: bell-shaped at the end of growing shoots; pale yellow with some red markings. Wonderful Autumn colour.

• Hard woody stem.

Epimedium grandiflorum
P. April–May.
Flowers: stems come up above the low ground-covering foliage with six to fifteen flowers per stem; star-like shape with little spur projection at back of flower; pale yellow, white and violet, and crimson tipped with white.

Eranthis
Winter Aconite. Tuber. Early Spring.
Flowers: yellow in a rosette of leaves on very short stem 7–10 cm (3–4 inches); useful for small moss gardens.

Eremurus
Foxtail Lily. P. * Early Summer.
Flowers: white and pale pink, pale yellow, and orange; thick fleshy stems vary in length from 60 cm to 2m (2–6 feet); long lasting and they take up interesting shapes after a day or two.

• Need a long drink in deep buckets.

Erica
Heaths and Heather. Low-growing E.S. * Most of the year. Very many different varieties. Useful in small arrangements. Can be used in small pots for gardens on a plate. Can be dried but does not last long as bells tend to drop off. *E. carnea, E. Cinerea, E. x darleyensis, E. gracilis, E. mediterranea. E. Vulgaris* syn. *Calluna vulgaris* is the Common Heather.

• Hammer woody stems.

Erigeron speciosus
Fleabane. P. Summer.

Flowers: daisy-type with a yellow centre disc and mauve or rosy pink outer petals.
● Remove all unwanted leaves immediately.

Erigeron

Eryngium amethystinum
P. * July–August.
Flowers: thistle-like; pretty amethyst colouring extends to stem and bracts; smaller flowers are pale blue; good for mixed summer arrangements and dried for winter use. Foliage is striking.

Eryngium

Escallonia
E.S. June–September.
Flowers: tiny trumpet-shaped in pinks and white; after the flowers have finished the small remaining seed heads can be used in a mixed green arrangement; long lasting. Foliage: small glossy leaves.
● Woody stems.

Eschsholzia
Californian Poppy. A. Summer.
Flowers: bright-coloured single cone-shaped poppy –

yellows, orange, scarlets, apricot, creams, white. Foliage is feathery.
● Put in water straight after curring.

Eschscholtzia californica

Eucalyptus
Gum Tree. E.T. * Most of the year.
Foliage: very useful and long lasting; pretty when treated with glycerine. Fruits are also good in dried arrangements.
● Hard woody stems.

Eucomis
Pineapple Flower. Bulb. * Autumn and Spring.
Flowers: green flower spike with purple markings. A novelty which always looks good for unusual groups.
● Soft fleshy stem.

Eucryphia glutinosa
Semi-E.S. July–August.
Flowers: often in pairs at the end of shoots; white with yellow anthers, about 5 cm (2 inches) diameter; like single roses.

Euonymus japonicus
E. and D.T. and S. * sometimes. All year except when new growth is soft in late Spring.
Foliage: range of variegation, excellent foliage for mixed greens and large arrangments. *E. europaeus* (Spindle Tree): deciduous, magnificent Autumn fruit. *E. radicans*: small-leafed.

Euphorbia
A. and P. * particularly *E.*

pulcherrima (Poinsettia) at Christmas. Greenhouse and garden varieties late Spring–Winter. *E. fulgens* is a good cut flower with long arching stems of small orange or white flowers, grown mostly in Holland and Kenya.
● All the family have stems which bleed and need sealing with a flame or boiling water.

Euphorbia

F

Fagus
Beech, D.T. * fresh and glycerined. Spring to Autumn.
Foliage: both green and copper forms are very valuable for backing foliage. The rare branches are good for the framework of shadow leaves (skeletonised magnolia).

Foeniculum vulgare
Fennel. P. Late Summer–mid Autumn.
Foliage: useful for large groups; seed heads good in mixed green arrangements.
● Hollow stem.

Forsythia
D.S. * February–April.

Flowers: one of the first shrubs to flower; forces well if brought into the house when just in bud; long lasting. Good forms are: *F. intermedia*, *F. ovata*, *F. suspensa*, *F. viridissima*.

Forsythia

Fothergilla major
D.S. April–May, Autumn.
Flowers: rather like off-white bottle brush flowers. Foliage: wonderful Autumn colour.

Freesia
Corm. * Nearly all year round.
Flowers: many beautiful colours, excellent flowers for small arrangements; some double forms are now available, such as 'Diane' white, 'Fantasy' cream.
● Cut stems and place in deep warm water if at all limp.

Freesia

Fritillaria
Bulb. * *F. imperialis* only. Spring.
A fairly large genus but only two species are commonly grown: *F. imperialis* (Crown Imperial) has a strong smell; useful for large arrangements and Dutch

groups but only available for a short time; long lasting. *F. meleagris* (Snake's Head Lily): good on its own or with other small flowers.

Fuchsia
D.S. * as a pot plant. Summer.
Flowers: very elegant when cut and used in vases with a foot – they must hang down to show well; quite long lasting.
● Split stem if woody.

Funkia
syn. *Hosta* (q.v.)

G

Gaillardia
Blanket Flower.
A. and P. * sometimes. July–September.
Flowers: yellow brown, rather like a helenium; long lasting; they lend themselves to simple mixed arrangements in baskets and heavy stoneware containers.

Gaillardia

Galanthus
Snowdrop. Bulb.
* January–February.
Flowers: white and some

green; double and single varieties, also a giant form; last well in water; pretty on their own in moss with ivy trails for foliage, or in little mixed posies.

Galega
Goat's Ruc. P. Summer.
Flowers: white or blue, member of the pea family; good for mixed arrangements.

Galtonia candicans
syn. *Hyacinthus candicans*. Summer Hyacinth. Bulb. July.
Flowers: white, long lasting, good for big groups; individual flowers can be used in a bouquet.
● Treat as soft succulent stems.

Gardenia
E.S. * sometimes. Late Summer.
Flowers: waxy white, highly scented; bruise very easily and go yellow-brown; excellent floating in a shallow crystal dish for a table decoration.
Foliage: glossy dark green.

Garrya elliptica
E.S. November–February. Catkins: silver-grey, male form has the longer catkins; long lasting in winter.
● Hard woody stems.

Garrya elliptica

Gaultheria
E.S. * Winter.
Foliage: dark green, long lasting. A number of species available–the most

useful have small-leafed arching sprays.

Gazania splendens
P. Summer–Autumn.
Flowers: colourful daisy-type in yellow, orange and browns; last well. Needs sun to flower well.
Foliage: silvery green with white underside.

Genista
D.S. * as a pot plant. Summer.
Flowers: yellow, long lasting, *G. hispanica* (Spanish Gorse) is good in the garden but not much use cut and is difficult to handle because of spines.
● Hard woody stems.

Gentiana
P. * Spring, September–October.
Many listed in catalogues but the main ones are *G. acaulis* (Spring), intense blue, short stiff stem; *G. sino-ornata* (September–October) deep blue, thin wiry stem, fine leaves; but not long lasting but lovely for small arrangements; do not use for decoration under artificial light as the blue colouring will be lost.

Geranium
see *Pelargonium*.

Gerbera jamesonii
Barberton Daisy. Pl.
* All year.
Flowers: daisy-type on long stems in wide range of colours; long lasting; good for modern arrangements.
Foliage: not often available.
● Seal cut stems straight away with a flame or boiling water.

Geum
P. Early Summer.
Flowers: simple and good for cottage-type arrangments; double and single forms; yellow and coppery red.
● Seal tips in a flame.

Gladiolus
Corm. * Summer.
Flowers: very wide range of colours; the small varieties are usually the best for arrangements; last well.
● Cut stems at an angle and remove basal leaves. Some people recommend taking the tip out of the flower stem to encourage the buds to open.

Gladiolus

Gloriosa
Torch Lily. Tuber.
* as a pot plant or a cut flower imported from Kenya. Summer.
Flowers: very decorative crimson red and yellow flowers on short stems from this climbing greenhouse plant; long lasting; good for exotic arrangements and combines well with fruit.
Foliage: each leaf ends in a tendril.
● Only cut single flower stems.

Godetia
A. * Summer.
Flowers: pretty cottage garden type, rather mallow-like in shape; colours from soft pinks and mauves to crimson.
● Clean off all unwanted foliage, stems may need crushing.

Grevillea
E.T. * Early Spring and Winter. *G. longifolia*: imported from France.
Foliage: often dyes but naturally it has silver and green rather long serrated leaves; fern-like appearance; can be pressed

in Autumn. *G. robusta*: used as a pot plant.

Gypsophila elegans
Baby's Breath. A. and P. *
Late Spring–early Autumn.
Flowers: attractive when arranged on their own and good for a hanging basket. *G. elegans*: single white flax-like flower. *G. paniculata* 'Bristol Fairy' is an excellent double form.
● Stems need hammering. Remove all foliage as it soon looks untidy.

Gypsophila

Halesia carolina
Snowdrop Tree. D.S.
May–June.
Flowers: very pretty white flowers; last well.
● Thin out leaves for a more dramatic effect. Hammer stems.

Hamamelis mollis
Witch Hazel. D.S.
* Autumn, Winter.
Flowers: fragrant flowers on bare stems in January and February are for Winter arrangements.
● Woody stems.

Hamamelis mollis

Hedera
Ivy. P. All year round.
Foliage: climbing and trailing, used extensively in flower arranging and floristry; very long lasting; some attractive variegated forms.

Helenium
P. * Late
Summer–Autumn.
Flowers: daisy-shaped, yellows to reddish browns; seed heads can be dried after flowering. Long lasting in water.

Helichrysum
Everlasting. A. * Summer.
Flowers: very important for drying; harvest when young for best results; dry by hanging upside down so stems become straight. Also sold as just flower heads to be glued on to false stems for arranging.

Helipterum roseum
A. * sometimes.
Summer.
Grown for drying which is carried out in the same way as for Helichrysum.

Helleborus
P. * November–June.
Range of colour from green, white, pinks to deep purple. Valuable group for the flower arranger. Flowers on single and compound stems.
● Treat tips with boiling water or burn and put straight into water. Some people recommend putting pin pricks all the way up the stem.

Helleborus

Hemerocallis
Day Lily. P.
June–September.
Flowers: cream and yellow to brown; flowers tend to open in the late afternoon and stay open until the next day; there are many flowers on each stem so there is a continuity of blooms.
Foliage: useful for mixed greens.

Heuchera
Coral Bells. P. May, late Autumn.
Flowers: useful dainty red flower spike.
Foliage: short-stemmed leaves go well with other flowers; pretty colouring in late Autumn.

Hosta

Hosta
syn. *Funkia*. P.
* April as pot plants,
May–August.
Foliage: excellent for the flower arranger with good variegated forms. Flowers: pale lilac, and of secondary importance. Interesting seed spikes for drying if flowers are not picked. The most useful forms are *H. fortunei* 'Marginato Alba',

H. glauca, *H. sieboldiana*.
● *Submerge if soft.*

Humulus
Hop. P. Summer.
Often found wild in hedgerows; very decorative and is ideal for Harvest Festival arrangements; dries well for Winter use.

Hyacinthus
Hyacinth. Bulb. * Early December–April/May.
Flowers: many different shades and colours and some double varieties, strongly scented and long lasting when cut; *H. orientalis albulus* (Roman Hyacinths) are the first to flower.
● Place cut hyacinths in a container on their own to allow the thick sap to exude from the stems before arranging with other flowers.

Hydrangea
D.S. * mostly as pot plants. Summer. Flowers: white, cream and green, blues, pinks; useful when fresh or dried. *H. macrophylla* is the most common, *H. paniculata* has pointed cream flower heads in September, *H. petiolaris* is a climber with white flowers.
● If flowers go limp, plunge under water for a few hours to revive. Dry only perfectly formed flowers.

Hydrangea

Hypericum
St. John's Wort. E. and D.S. Summer, Autumn.
Flowers: range from pale yellow to deep buttercup

colour; many named varieties; long flowering period. Foliage and seed capsule are good in Autumn.
● Remove lower leaves and hammer the stems of the taller shrubs.

Iberis
Candytuft. A. and P. * very occasionally.
Late Spring and Summer.
Flowers: white, pinks, mauves; good in simple mixed summer arrangements; annual type have interesting seed heads which dry well; perennial types have woody stems.

Ilex
Holly. E.T. * Cut foliage in December.
Berries: red, orange and yellow berried forms are the most interesting, berries are carried only by females. Foliage: some good variegated forms, many different shaped leaves.
● Keep cut holly in a damp place but do not put stems in water for too long as it tends to drop its leaves when cut and standing in water; if picked in advance, store where birds and mice cannot reach the berries.

Ipomoea
syn. *Pharbitis*.
Morning Glory. A. * as a pot plant.
Summer.
Flowers: blue, last only a very short time.

● Place tips in boiling water for a few seconds before arranging.

Iris
Bulbs and tubers.
* Winter, Spring, early Summer.
Flowers: divided botanically into eleven groups, covering a wide range of different shapes and sizes. The main ones are listed below:
I. pseudocorus (Flag Iris): short flowering season (May–June) but good seed pods and useful foliage. *I. xiphium* (Dutch, English and Spanish Iris): commercial iris in pale and dark blue, yellow, white and now a few in bronze are available. *I tuberosa* (Widow Iris), sometimes listed as Hermodactylus tuberosus: a good small iris for arranging. *I. unguicularis* syn. *I. stylosa*: first iris of the season, cut when in bud; foliage untidy but flowers go well with jasmine and Christmas roses. *I. reticulata* (Dwarf Iris) and *I. germanica* (Common or Bearded Iris) are the garden iris.

Iris

Ixia
Corm. * May–September.
Flowers: attractive spike – habit and foliage like a baby gladiolus; white and blue and violet; very long lasting.
● Cut stems may need hammering.

Jasminum
Semi-E. and D.S.
* *J. polyanthum* as a pot plant. Most of the year. Not long lasting when cut, but flower buds keep opening. *J. nudiflorum* (Winter Jasmine) D. has yellow flowers on long bare stems from November–February. *N. officinale* (Common jasmine) semi-E. has very fragrant white flowers from June–September. *J. primulinum* E. has yellow flowers March–April.
● Dip stem tips in boiling water.

Jasminum

Juniperus
E.T. Nearly all year.
Foliage: used by florists for wreath work but can be good in mixed green arrangements, especially when bearing cones.

Kalenchoe
Pot plant. *
December–March, June–July.
Flowers: coral or cream in large form (June–July), small flat-headed plants have bright red and cream flowers in Winter which last well when cut. Used a lot in planted arrangements.
● Split stems.

Kalmia
Calico Bush. E.S. or T. *
May–June.
Flowers: very pretty pink flowers, look like icing sugar flowers.

Kentranthus
Sometimes spelt Centranthus. Valerian. P. Summer.
Flowers: usually pink but also available in white and a deep rose; last well.

Kerria japonica
D.S. Spring.
Flowers: single or double flowers on long stems with fine foliage. Long lasting when cut. Bare branches useful in Winter months – not unlike Dogwood.

Kniphofia uvaria
Red Hot Poker. P.
* July–October.
Flowers: take up elegant curves when in water and last well.
Foliage: untidy.
● Soft fleshy stems.

L

Lachenalia aloides
Cape Bowslip. Bulb.
* March–April.
Flowers: green, red and yellow small flower spikes; long lasting.

Lamium
Dead Nettle. P. Late Spring, Summer.
Foliage: more important than flowers; like a short mauve/ pink coloured nettle; pretty in small arrangements.

Larix decidua
Larch. D.T. * Spring, Winter
This is the only deciduous cone-bearing tree. Foliage: attractive in young form in Spring. Lasts well in water. Cones: on bare branches in Winter. Also excellent when dead and covered with lichen.
● Put tips of young growth in boiling water.

Lathyrus

Lathyrus
Sweet Pea. A. * April (greenhouse) – August.
Flowers: pastel shades, not long lasting; best arranged on their own or with a clean cut foliage.
● Never spray the petals

unless it is very hot so they will dry quickly – the petals spot and go papery if left wet for a long period. Stems may need splitting if very woody.

Laurus nobilis
Bay. E.S. April–May.
Foliage: a useful aromatic foliage with interesting green flowers in late Spring.

Lavandula
Lavender. P. * Summer.
Flowers: purple spikes with fine scent.
Foliage: silver-grey. Not cut a great deal for arrangements but it is a useful shape of leaf and flower stem for a small vase.

Lavatera
Mallow. A. Summer.
Flowers: pink and white, not long lasting but buds open well in water; good for large mixed Summer arrangements.

Leontopodium
Edelweiss. P. June–July.
Flowers: silver and grey, ideal to arrange with gentians in a very small vase or on a pewter plate with crystal.

Leucocoryne
Glory of the Sun. B. * Late Spring.
Flowers: a form of small lily; pale blue/purple flower spike on stems of 30 cm (1 foot); very fragrant.

Leucojum
Summer Snowflake. Bulb.
May–June.
Flowers: green and white, ideal for medium-sized arrangements.

Leycesteria formosa
D.S. June–September.
Flowers: purple, last quite well. Remove some leaves to show flowers and bracts.

Liatris
P. * Spring and Summer.

Flowers: rose and purple stiff spikes, imported from Holland.
● Stems are very firm and need hammering. Rub off the basal foliage.

Ligustrum
Privet. Mostely E.S. * foliage. Summer and Winter.
Foliage: golden form is good in mixed green and Summer arrangements.
Berries: black, useful for Winter arrangements.
● Hammer stems.

Lilium

Lilium
True Lily. Bulb.
* Most of the year. A vast group of flowering plants which last well and make a bold centre to a large group. The main colours are white, yellow, orange and pink. Large numbers are forced in Holland to supply the flower markets. *L. auratum:* July–October; cream and white flowers with yellow and brown spotted petals and a yellow throat – the pollen stains badly so anthers should be removed. *L. candidum* (Madonna Lily): June–July; probably the best known of all lilies; old fashioned upright stems of sweet smelling white waxy petalled flowers, excellent in mixed Summer arrangements; long lasting.
● Remove small leaves which would be below the water line when arranged. Split stems and place in deep buckets for support.

Limonium
Sea Lavender, Statice. P. *

Summer, dried in Winter.
Flowers: everlasting and more useful dried in Winter than as a cut flower in Summer; tiny deep purple and blue flowers rather like a perennial gypsophila. *L. suworowii* A. * May–June.
Flowers: long lilac spike with side branches at base.
Foliage: no foliage on stems but flower spikes come from a rosette of leaves.

Linaria
Toadflax. A. and P. July onwards.
Flowers: similar to small antirrhinums, on stems 30–45 cm (12–18 ins).

Linum
Flax. A. * sometimes.
June–July.
Flowers: blue on delicate stem; useful for mixed Summer arrangements.

Lobelia cardinalis
Cardinal Flower. P.
Summer.
Flowers and foliage: superb red up to 90 cm (3 ft) tall; excellent for mixed red arrangements; last well.
● May require hot water treatment.

Lonicera
Honeysuckle. E. and D.S. Summer and late Winter. *L. fragrantissima:* late Winter. *L. periclymenum:* May–August; sweet smelling and long lasting if cut in bud. *L. nitida* is a useful evergreen foliage with small round deep green leaves. Does not often flower.

Lunaria
Honesty. B. * Seed head form in Autumn and Winter.
Flowers: violet and lilac colour. Seed heads; very important but must be harvested before seed pod central membrane becomes stained from the seeds; seed pods are often dyed.
● Hang upside down to dry.

Lupinus polyphyllus
Lupin. P. * occasionally.
May–June.
Flowers: variety of colours,
good on their own or for
mixed Summer
arrangements.
● Fill hollow stems with
water and plug. This will
increase their life by one or
two days and encourage the
stems to take up elegant
curves.

Lychnis
syn. *Agrostemma*
Campion. P. Summer.
L. chalcedonica: scarlet
flowers.
L. coronaria: white woolly
shoots at base and on the
purple-coloured flower
spike.
● Soft stem treatment
unless stems are old and
woody; both varieties are
long lasting.

Macleaya
syn. *Bocconia*. Plume
Poppy. P. Summer.
Foliage: silver and grey
with insignificant fluffy
pink/cream flowers in July.
● Seal stem tips in boiling
water before use.

Magnolia
D.T. Late Spring and
Summer.
Flowers: cream and white,
and purple; blossom is
usually out before foliage
and is subject to frost
damage in late Spring; best
arranged on their own. *M.
soulangeana* (April): white
with purple flowers. *M.
stellata*: first to flower,

Magnolia

March–April: star-shaped
flowers. *M. grandiflora*
(August–October): large
water-lily type flowers.
● Woody stems. The leaves
of *M. grandiflora* are
excellent dried for Winter
use. Harvest in the
Autumn and press under
the carpet.

Mahonia
E.S. Autumn and Winter.
Foliage: good colour in
Autumn.
Flowers: Winter and early
Spring, very fragrant and
used in small
arrangements. *M. beali* and
M. 'Charity' are excellent
forms.

Malcolmia maritima
Virginia Stock. A.
Early Summer to Autumn.
Flowers: very dainty and
sweetly scented; suitable
for small arrangements.
● Hammer stems if hard.

Malus
Flowering Crab. D.S.
Spring and Autumn.
Wide range of flowering
trees, notable species are
M. floribunda and *M.
atrosanguinea*.

Matthiola
Brompton Stock. B.
* Spring and Autumn.
Flowers: many shades from
white, cream, soft pinks,
mauves, purples and
apricot on stiff stems with
green and grey foliage; last
well.
● Stems very woody and
need hot water treatment.
No foliage must go in
water; the stems are smelly

Mathiola

so it is a good idea to change
the water frequently.

Megasea
syn. *Bergenia* (q.v.)

Molucella laevis
Bells of Ireland. A.
* Summer and in dried
form.
Flowers: the flowers
themselves are
insignificant and it is the
calyx that is the decorative
part: useful in green
arrangements and long
lasting.
● Warm water treatment if
soft. Removal all the
leaves.

Monarda didyma
Balm. P. June–September.
Flowers: decorative scarlet
flowers, good in mixed
garden arrangements.

Muscari
Grape Hyacinth. Bulb.
* March–April.
Flowers: useful small blue
flower which is long lasting
and good in small
arrangements.
Foliage: very untidy and
only the foliage of *M.
latifolium* is used.
● Soft stems; always
remove any white part
when cutting stems.

Myosotis
Forget-me-not. P.
* Spring and Summer.
Flowers: pretty
old-fashioned flowers
which are ideal for small
baskets and vases of mixed
Spring and Summer
flowers.
● Once they have taken up

water they last well, but
the leaves must be soaked
first; remove many of the
leaves.

Narcissus

Narcissus
Daffodil. Bulb. * Early
November–May.
Flowers: many varieties
available; best arranged as
a mixture of different types
with their own foliage and
a little background foliage
of such things as hazel and
berberis; scented named
varieties include 'Pheasant
Eye' and 'Cheerfulness';
miniature narcissi are good
for small arrangements –
*N. bulbicodium, N.
cyclamineus, N. jonquilla,
N. juncifolius*.

Nemesia strumosa
A. * as pot plants.
Summer.
Flowers: bright colours,
ideal for small
arrangements and last
quite well.

Nepeta
Catmint. (Nettle family) P.
May–September.
Flowers: pale lavender

flower spikes.
Foliage: silver and grey.
Very useful in mixed
garden baskets.
● Stems may need crushing
to take up water.

Nerine
Guernsey Lily. Bulb.
* Autumn.
Flowers: hybrids are now
produced in wonderful
colours from white, pale
pink, through to coral and
scarlet; the old *N. bowdenii*
in hard pink is the main
commercial variety; all
wonderful in arrangements
and long lasting.
● Soft fleshy stems.

Nerine

Nicotiana affinis
Tobacco Plant. A.
Summer.
Flowers: lime green and
white forms are the most
useful; flowers do not last
long but buds open well in
water and will replace
flowers as they go over;
ideal for mixed Summer
groups and mixed green
arrangements.
● Stems may need
crushing. Remove all
foliage at and below the
water line.

Nicotiana

Nigella
Love-in-the-Mist. A.
* Summer.
Flowers: shades of blue and
white in a collar of feathery
greenery; excellent seed
heads at the end of the
season which dry well; not
long lasting but buds open
in water. Remove foliage
from near water line. *N.
damascena* is a good form.

Nigella

Nymphaea
Water Lily. P.
Summer.
Flowers: make an
attractive table
arrangement in a shallow
dish but are not easy to
obtain.
● Keep stems and leaves
right down in water. To
keep the flowers open,
paraffin wax must be
dropped into the base of the
petals – it should be at just
the right temperature to
run into the base of the
stem and then set firmly. If
too hot it will damage the
petals.

O

Oenothera biennis
Evening Primrose. B.

July–September.
Flowers: buds will open
well in water but flowers
are not long lasting and are
best used in the latter part
of the day. The buds open
freely as the open flowers
fade.
● Hammer any stems that
are woody.

Olearia haastii
New Zealand Daisy Bush.
E.S. July–August
(flowers), all year (foliage).
Foliage: dark green with
silver back to leaf.
Flowers: white daisy-like
flowers with yellow disc;
sweet smelling.
● Woody stems.

Onopordon acanthium
Cotton Thistle. P.
Summer.
Flowers: purple-flowered
heads but they are prickly
so cruel to handle.
● Put stem tip in very hot
water and give a good drink
before arranging.

Ornithogalum

Ornithogalum
Bulb. * sometimes.
Spring and early Summer.
O. thyrsoides
(Chincherinchee): white,
sometimes imported at
Christmas; long lasting. *O
nutans*: green and white
bell-shaped flower in April
and May. *O. umbellatum*
(Star of Bethlehem): white
star-like flowers with
green and white backs.
● As tips of stems become
soft, recut – should last a
long time in water. Flowers
from South Africa may
have tips of stem waxed. Cut
off and place in warm water.

Osmanthus delavayi
E.S. April.
Flowers: small fragrant
white flowers on stiff
small-leaved branches,
long lasting. *O. ilicifolius* is
a dark foliage with small
holly-like leaves.

Osmunda regalis
Royal Fern. P.
Autumn.
Foliage: excellent Autumn
colouring but it is best
dried for Winter use,
pressed under a carpet.

P

Paeonia
Peony. P. and D.S.
* May–June.
Flowers: white, pink, reds
in single or double form,
must be picked in bud if
they are to last in water;
often cold-stored to extend
their flowering period; tree
paeonies are slow growing
and should only be used for
special decorations or
Japanese style
arrangements.
Foliage: good Autumn
colour on old leaves.
● Split woody stems. Young
foliage can be floated in a
bath.

Paeonia

Papaver
Poppy. A. and P.
P. nudicaule Late
Spring–early Autumn.
P. orientale: unusual shdes
and good for large groups.
P. nudicaule (Iceland
Poppy): colourful reds,
orange, yellow, cream and
white. *P. rhoeas* (Shirley)
and *P. somniferum*
(Opium) are in softer
shades and usually carry
more petals.
● Pick when just showing a
trace of colour and burn
tips of stems immediately.

Papaver

Passiflora caerulea
Passion Flower. Climber. *
sold as pot plants in shops.
Summer.
Flowers: striking but do not
last long, especially if
stems are short; best
floating in a shallow dish.
Foliage: young shoots are
attractive and have
tendrils attached.
● Split flower stems.

Pelargonium

Pelargonium
Geranium. P. * pot plants.
Summer.
Flowers: pinks, reds,
mauves and white. Foliage:

small shoots are good for
mixed green arrangements
or in a goblet of mixed
flowers.
● Split stems.

Penstemon
P. Summer.
Flowers: reds, pink and
white similar to a small
foxglove.
● Stems may need
splitting.

Penstemon

Pernettya mucronata
E.S. Early Summer
(flowers), Autumn
(berries).
Berries: white or pink.
Flowers: only on some
varieties, and are like
small sprays of
lily-of-the-valley.

Petasites fragrans
Winter Heliotrope. P.
Early Spring.
Flowers: Vanilla scented;
spikes are useful,
particularly the
green-flowered form *P.
japonicus giganteus*.
● Soak foliage before use if
it is soft.

Petunia
A. * as a pot plant.
Summer.
Flowers: good colour range
and useful for a mixed
Summer basket but lasting
qualities are poor.
● Arrange in warm water.

Phalaris
Ribbon Grass or Gardener's
Garters.
P. Summer.
Decorative grass, quite
pretty when young and
growing spikes are used in

conjunction with early
Spring flowers, not long
lasting in water.
● Try putting tips in warm
water.

Pharbitis
syn. *Ipomoea* (q.v.)

Philadelphus coronarius
Mock Orange. D.S.
June–July.
Flowers: some varieties
have masses of white
flowers which are highly
scented. Range of flower
size and shape. Two good
varieties are *P. 'Belle
Etoile'* and *P. 'Virginal'*. *P.
coronarius aureus* has
excellent bright yellow
foliage in Spring.

Philadelphus

Phlomis fruticosa
Jerusalem Sage. E.S.
June.
Flowers: pale yellow
colouring and rather like a
stinging nettle flower.

Phlox

Phlox
A. and P. Summer.
P. drummondii (A.): long
lasting in water and very
colourful, self-coloured,
bi-coloured and

tri-coloured, usually
available July–September.
P. paniculata and *P. x
hortorum* (P.) have a sweet
scent in early Autumn;
many pink and mauve
shades and white; last well;
stems woody.

Phormium tenax
New Zealand Flax. P.
Summer
Foliage: very striking
spear-shaped leaf up to 2
metres (7 ft) long; good for
large arrangements or
mixed greens. *P. tenax
variegatum* has a striped
yellow and green leaf. *P.
tenax veitchii* has creamy
white stripes.

Phygelius capensis
Cape Figwort. E.S.
Late Summer.
Flowers: scarlet flowers
make interesting material
for a red group.
● Split stems and stand in
warm water.

Phygelius capensis

Physalis franchetii
Chinese Lantern. P. * fresh
or dried. Early Summer
(fresh).
Ideal for drying for Winter
decoration but can be used
in its fresh state.
● Remove most of the
leaves.

Phsostegia virginiana
Obedient Plant. P. *
August–September.
Flowers: purple or white,
long lasting; can be placed
in certain positions on the
stem and will remain there,
hence the plant's common
name.

• Woody stems, remove many of the leaves up the square stem.

Phytolacca
Red Ink Plant. P.
Late Summer.
Berries: dark purple and stain badly; berries and roots are poisonous. May be used in its early stage when green or later when coloured.
• Remove most of the leaves.

Pieris floribunda syn. *Andromeda floribunda.*
Lily-of-the-Valley Tree. E.S.
* March–May.
Flowers: Like lily-of-the-valley sprays. *P. japonica* has larger sprays. *P. formosa* has young scarlet growth at the tips of foliage. Foliage lasts well.

Pinus
Pine. E.T. * sometimes.
Autumn and Winter.
Cones: branches carrying cones are very useful for Winter decorations. Many different forms and a wide colour range. The blue is the most popular.

Pittosporum tenuifolium
E.T. * October–April.
Foliage: long lasting glossy small round leaves with wavy edges; important commercial crop.

Platycodon

Platycodon grandiflorus
Chinese Bell Flower.
P. Summer.
Flowers: white and blue; stem lengths up to 60 cm (2 feet).

• Stems tend to bleed – seal in a flame and get them into water straight away.

Polygonatum multiflorum
Solomon's Seal. P.
* May to June.
Foliage: arching stems carrying little tubular white and green flowers; long lasting in water. The

Polygonatum

leaves can be used on their own after the flowers have finished.
• Cut at an angle and allow a deep drink before use.

Polygonum baldschuanicum
Russian Vine. D. Climber.
July–October.
Flowers: small sprays of flowers can be cut and used in candle cup arrangements.
• Soak well before use.

Potentilla fruticosa
E.S. June–August.
Flowers: small yellow single rose-like; last well.
• Hammer woody stems.

Primula
P. * March–June and Autumn.
Popular garddern plants are *P. auricula, P. denticulata, P. japonica* and *P. polyanthus.*
• *P. polyanthus* sometimes wilt so get into deep water straight away and prick right down the stem. *P. auricula* and *P. denticulata* normally take up water well.

Primula

Prunus
Plum, Cherry, Peach and Apricot. D.T.
Spring (flowers), Autumn (fruit). *P. laurocerasus* (E.) is the Common Laurel. *P. subhirtilla autumnalis* flowers in October–November.

Prunus

Pulmonaria officinalis
Jerusalem Cowslip, Soldiers and Sailors.
P. Spring.
Flowers: pink, turning to a purple-blue; often used in mixed Spring arrangements with primroses, polyanthus, heathers; quite long lasting. Foliage: spotted.

Pulsatilla vulgaris
syn. *Anemone pulsatilla.*
Pasque Flower.
P. Spring, Early Summer.
Flowers: pale mauve; *P. alpina sulphurea* has pale yellow flowers in May and June. Seed head attractive with mixed greens.
• Place flowers in deep water before arranging.

Pyracantha
Firethorn. E.S. May

(flowers), Autumn (berries). Flowers: white. Berries: red, orange-yellow and will last all Winter.
• Woody stems and remove spiteful thorns.

Pyracantha

Pyrethrum
A form of Chrysanthemum. P.
* Early Summer.
Flowers: single-daisy type in red and pink with yellow centre disc; quite long lasting.

Pyrethrum

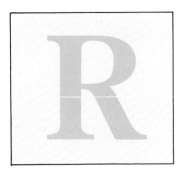

R

Ranunculus
Buttercup family. P.
* Spring and Summer.
Flowers: many bright colours; good for arrangements and long

Ranunculus

lasting; as flowers open, the weight makes them take up attractive curves. *R. asiaticus* is the usual commercial flower.
● Allow plenty of water as the heads are heavy and can fracture stems if they bend over when limp.

Reseda
Mignonette. P.
June–October.
Flowers: green and yellow with a little white, look rather like millet; they are sweet-scented and used to feature in tied nosegays.

Rheum palmatum
Rhubarb family.
P. Summer.
Foliage; large leaves used in very big groups. Flowers: like the wild dock in deep red; not often grown.
● Submerge leaves before use as they easily become soft.

Rhododendron

Rhododendron and Azalea
E. and D.S.
November–August.
Important group of shrubs and trees, wide range of colours in white, cream,

pale yellow, pinks, reds and purples; last up to ten days if cut in bud.

Rhus cotinus
Smoke Tree. D.S.
Autumn.
Foliage: useful colour and has a smoke-grey effect from the spent flower stems in Autumn. *R. typhina* (Stag's Horn Sumach): pyramidal flower panicles, wonderful Autumn colour.

Ribes
Flowering Currant.
D.S. Spring.
R. sanguineum: flowers in deep pink, hang down like clusters of grapes before much of the foliage has opened; long lasting but it has a strong unpleasant smell when cut in the house. There are named varieties with white and yellow flowers in this species.
● Treat as woody stems.

Rodgersia pinnata
P. June–July.
Flowers: white or rose pink with flat heads.
● Hollow stem.

Romneya

Romneya
P. Summer.
Flowers: like a large single white poppy with grey-green foliage, sometimes mistaken for a paeony.

Rosa
D.S. May–July and Autumn (garden), all year round (commercial crop). Many different varieties, forms and colours.

Rosa

Important as a garden flower, commercial crop, and excellent for the flower arranger.
● Remove thorns except for a single rose in a specimen vase, cut and hammer stems, and put stem tips in boiling water. Recut and repeat treatment if they show signs of wilting.

Rosmarinus officinalis
Rosemary. E.S. * sometimes.
Summer and Autumn.
Foliage: silver grey back to dark green narrow leaves, very fragrant.

Rudbeckia
P. July–September.
Flowers: yellow and brown colours, daisy like, long lasting when cut. Most common forms are *R. hirta* (Black-eyed Susan) and *R. laciniata* (Cone Flower).
● Hammer thick stems.

Rudbeckia

Ruscus aculeatus
Butcher's Broom. E.S. * dried and dyed.
Rarely used in its natural form. Female plants are attractive when carrying berries.

Ruta graveolens
Rue. E.S. Summer.
Foliage: small and useful in pretty green and grey colouring; smell is sometimes thought to be unpleasant. Flowers: not significant but can be used. Young foliage is best in May–October.

Salix
Willow. D.T. * Late Winter, early Spring.
S. babylonica (Weeping Willow): beautiful in Spring when just breaking. *S. medemii:* excellent for early catkings. Pussy willow bare branches are very popular during late Winter. *S. matsudana* 'Tortuosa' (Contorted Willow) is often grown for use in early Spring.

Salpiglossis sinuata
A. Summer.
Flowers: colourful and resemble the convolvulus flower in shape; good for mixed arrangements.

Salvia
Sage. A. and P. * as a pot plant.
Summer.
Flowers: red, and blue and purple. Foliage: strongly scented soft grey and green. Good forms are: *S. sclarea* (Clary), *S. splendens* (Scarlet Sage).

Sansevieria
Mother-in-law's Tongue.
Pot plant.
* All year.
A leaf will last well in an

arrangement and can take the place of an iris or phormium leaf in a mixed green group. Leaves have attractive markings.

Santolina
Lavender Cotton. E.S.
July.
Foliage: silver-grey with yellow flower heads in July; rather a pungent smell.
● Place in water straight away as it wilts quickly; plunge before use for a few hours if necessary.

Scabiosa

Scabiosa
Scabious. A. and P.
* Summer.
S. caucasia (P.) are blues and sometimes white form. *S. atropurpurea* (A.) are a wide range of blue, purple and deep red, and last well in water. *S. elata* syn. *Cephalaria tatarica* is the yellow perennial scabious and is also useful.

Schizanthus
Poor Man's Orchid. A.
May–August.
Pretty foliage and a wide range of flower colours.

Schizostylis

Schizostylis
Kaffir Lily. P.
* Autumn.
Members of the iris family.
S. 'Viscountess Byng' (pink) is the main form.

Scilla
Bluebell and Wild Hyacinth. Bulb.
* sometimes. Late Spring.
Flowers: useful for small arrangements in late Spring but do not last long.

Sedum
P. * Summer and Autumn.
Large group of rock garden plants, the most popular varieties are: *S. sieboldii* 'Medio-variegatum': round flat fleshy leaves with a yellow blotch, useful for small arrangements.
S. spectabile atropurpureum 'Brilliant' has excellent large pink flower heads in Autumn.

Sedum

Sempervivum
Houseleek.
P. Summer.
Foliage: rosette of thick fleshy leaves can be used to good effect in the centre of a small mixed green.
Flowers: star-like, can be useful for a special arrangement.

Senecio laxifolius
E.S. All year round except January and February.
Foliage: silver-grey with white backs to the leaves.
Flowers: yellow daisy-like on silvery spikes. July. *S. cineraria* syn. *Cineraria maritima* (q.v.)

Sidalcea
Mallow family.
P. Summer.
Flowers: pink and purple.
Foliage: pretty for a mixed Summer arrangement.

Silybum
Milk Thistle.
B. Summer.
Foliage: beautifully marked.
Flowers: rose and purple in Summer.
● Leaves need boiling water treatment. It is a good idea to float them in a bowl of water before use.

Smilacina racemosa
P. May.
Foliage: similar to Solomon's Seal.
Flowers: feathery cluster at the end of the leaf spike; fragrant.

Solanum capsicastrum
Winter Cherry. P. * as a pot plant.
Winter.
Berries: red; flowers must be pollinated by August if berries are to form and ripen for Christmas. Remove a few leaves to allow berries to show to advantage.
● Woody stem.

Solidago
Golden Rod. P.
August–September.
Flowers: arching sprays of yellow flowers which can vary in colour if a range of varieties is grown; seed heads are also useful.
● Woody stems. Remove many of the lower leaves.

Sorbus
D.T. Spring and Autumn.
S. aria (Whitebeam): beautiful silver foliage in April and May, and good Autumn fruit; the elegant branches last well when cut. *S. aucuparia* (Rowan or Mountain Ash): good Autumn fruit.

Spartium junceum
Spanish Broom. D.S.

June–September.
Flowers: yellow pea-shaped flowers similar to common broom but larger and less crowded. Lasts well when cut.
● Hammer stems.

Spiraea
D.S. Spring and June–September.
Wide range of foliage and flowers: *S. arguta: white, April–May. S. douglasii:* purple and rose, June–July. *S. japonica:* rose and red, June–July. *S. veitchii:* white flowers, long arching branches, June–July.

Stachys lanata
Lamb's Ears, Lamb's Tongue.
P. June.
Foliage: low growing with soft grey felty leaves which can be used for most of the year. Flowers: flower spike is useful for extra length on foliage stem just before it opens in July and it can be dried.
● Do not allow foliage to become soaked or it will act as a syphon. Tips may be burnt.

Stephanotis
Madagascar Jasmine.
P. * April–November.
Flowers: wax-like tubular and star-shaped white flowers with a very strong smell; long lasting; good for table bowl decorations where short stems are required.

Symphoricarpos
Snowberry. D.S.
* Autumn.
Foliage: oval-shaped leaves

RIGHT: A flat fruit dish with a collection of Midsummer flowers, including *Kentranthus ruber, Delphinium, Alchemilla, Digitalis, Dianthus barbatus, Rosa* Columbine and R. Magenta, *Campanula, Erigeron, Phlomis, Escallonia, Lupinus* and *Aquilegia.*

Symphoricarpos rivularis

on arching sprays with opaque berries at the tips in white or pink. The variety 'Constance Spry' is excellent. Lasts extremely well in water.

Syringa

Syringa
Lilac. D.S. * May–June and forced from Holland, December–March.
Flowers: white, pink and mauve, lilac, deep purple.
● Woody stems, remove all leaves from flower stem but keep some short foliage shoots to arrange in amongst the bare stems.

Tagetes
African and French

Marigolds. * African Marigolds on single stems up to 30 cm (12 inches). Summer.
Flowers: orange, yellow, brown and have a strong smell which can be unpleasant in the house.
● Cut stems, remove basal leaves and place in warm water.

Tagetes

Taxus
Yew. E.T.
Autumn–Winter.
Foliage: useful backing for large groups in Winter months; long lasting; attractive variegated form. Berries are poisonous.
● Hammer well.

Thalictrum dipterocarpum
Meadow Rue.
P. Summer.
Foliage: very attractive for mixed garden flower arrangements, similar to quilegia; *T. dipterocarpum* 'Hewitt's Double' is attractive but a little untidy and is best used in small pieces.

Tilia
Lime. D.T. Spring.
Foliage: young lime is very beautiful in Spring as background foliage and stripped lime is excellent – remove all the leaves from the branches so that just the flowers and bracts remain. Popular forms are *T. europaea* (Common Lime) and *T. petiolaris* (Pendant Silver Lime).

Tradescantia
P. * *T. fluminensis*

(Wandering Jew).
Summer.
Foliage: coloured forms in silver, purple and gold are the most popular. Flowers: rather insignificant and not widely used. The herbaceous plant *T. virginiana* has useful flower stems in July and August but foliage is not good for arranging.

Tritonia
Montbretia. Corm.
May–June.
Flowers: mostly orange colours; long lasting.
Foliage: iris-like.
● Place cut stems in deep water.

Trollius

Trollius europaeus
Globe Flower.
P. * Early June.
Flowers: yellow like a giant buttercup, not long lasting but a good shape and foliage is interesting.
● Cut when young and get into water straight away.

Tropaeolum majus

Tropaeolum majus
Nasturtium. A.
Summer.
Flowers: good colours and

last quite well when cut; best varieties are those with double flowers.

Tulipa
Tulip. Bulb.
* December–May.
Flowers: wide range of colours; flowers take up beautiful curves in water; lily-flowered and double tulips are very useful.
● Wrap flowers in stiff paper and give a long drink to ensure that flower heads do not droop and break the delicate stem. Some people recommend pricking through the stem under the flower head with a pin to enable tulips to take up water better.

Typha
Reed Mace, Bulrush.
P. * Autumn for seed heads.
Foliage: useful for backing large Summer groups.
Flowers: brown cylindrical head.
● Cut flower before it is really ripe and spray with hair lacquer to stop it splitting.

V

Vallota speciosa
Scarborough Lily. Bulb. * sometimes.
September–October.
Flowers: three or four scarlet flowers at the top of the thick fleshy stem; similar to a small Amaryllis; long lasting.
● Thick fleshy stems.

Verbascum
Mullein. B. June onwards.
Flowers: interesting flower

spike with pale yellow flowers on a thick hairy stem; useful in mixed Summer groups. Foliage: large hairy soft leaves.
● Put in warm water if it begins to wilt. The seed heads dry well if hung upside down and being tall they make a useful backing for arrangements.

Verbena
A. and P. Summer.
Flowers: good colour range in the annual form. Flowers: flat heads, long lasting and good for mixed Summer groups; best perennial forms are *V. bonariensis* and *V. canadensis*.
● *Split stems if at all woody.*

Veronica
syn. *Hebe* in shrubby form. E.S. form and P. border plants.
Summer. Very large genus. Foliage: wide range of leaf shape and colour, useful for mixed greens; the smallest form *V. buchananii* is one of the most useful species. Flowers: loose spikes of blue, pale pinks or white colouring.
● Woody stems.

Viburnum
Snowball Tree, Wayfaring Tree. D.S. and T. All year round from different varieties.
Flowers: fragrant, usually white or pink in flat heads; some early flowers catch the frost. Foliage: takes good colour in Autumn. Best hybrids are *V. x bodnantense*, *V. x burkwoodii*, and best species are *V. carlesii*, *V. fragrans* and *V. opulus* (Guelder Rose).

Vinca
Periwinkle. Pl. Late Spring.
Foliage: long trailing stems of oval leaves with yellow markings; variegated form is useful. Flowers: blue; of secondary importance.
● Split stems.

Viola

Viola
Violet. P. * 'Princess of Wales' (September–October) and 'Herrick' (March–April) only.
Flowers: garden varieties of viola are useful for table bowls and small vases. *V. tricolor* is the plant that the garden pansy has been derived from. When cut it can only be used for small posies.
● *V. odorata* (True Violet) drink through their heads and should always be kept moist.

Viscum album
Mistletoe. P. (parasitic). * Winter.
Useful at Christmas; it looks attractive just glittered with variegated holly and ivy in a low bowl. It is unwise to encourage mistletoe in the garden as it will kill trees.

Vitis
Vine. P. Autumn.
Foliage: interesting shaped leaves with good colour in Autumn (Autumn colour comes at the end of their life). *V. coignetiae* is recommended.
● Dip tips of leaves in boiling water, but leaves do not last long.

Watsonia
Corm. August–September.
Flowers: very elegant spikes, like a fine flowered gladiolus, white and pale pink with some scarlet and crimson.
● As *Gladiolus*.

Wisteria
Climber.
Late Spring–early Summer.
Lasts only a very short time when cut. Needs to be used in a vase on a stem so that the flowers hang down.
● Place tips in boiling water to hold flowers.

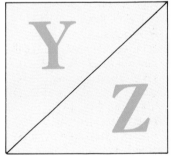

Ycca
E.S. Summer.
Flowers: useful for a really striking large group. Foliage: individual leaves can be cut to take the place of large Phormium or Cordyline.

Zantedeschia aethiopica
syn. *Calla aethiopica*. Arum Lily, Lords and Ladies. P. *
December–April, outdoor crop July–August.
Flowers: green form is very popular; the yellow *Z. elliotiana* and the little pink and cream Arum *Z. rehmanii* are imported, usually in Spring.
● Soft fleshy stem.

Zinnia

Zinnia elegans
A. Summer–Autumn.
Flowers: good colours; subject to heads bending over at the top of the flower stem. This flower is sometimes wired internally when purchased from the florist to hold the heavy flower head in position.
● Place tips in hot water then give a good drink in warm water before arranging. In large varieties the stem is hollow and should be filled with warm water.

Cross reference chart

Cross reference chart
Common names to Latin genera

African Lily	*Agapanthus*
Alder	*Alnus*
Angel's Trumpet	*Datura*
Apricot	*Prunus*
Artichoke	*Cynara*
Arum Lily	*Zantedeschia*
Ash, Mountain	*Sorbus*
Aster, China	*Callistephus*
Autumn Crocus	*Colchicum*
Baby's Breath	*Gypsophila*
Balm	*Monarda*
Bamboo	*Arundinaria*
Barberry	*Berberis*
Barberton Daisy	*Gerbera*
Bay	*Laurus*
Bear's Breeches	*Acanthus*
Beech	*Fagus*
Bell Flower, Chinese	*Platycodon*
Belladonna Lily	*Amaryllis*
Bellflower	*Campanula*
Bells of Ireland	*Molucella*
Birch	*Betula*
Bird of Paradise	*Strelitzia*
Black-eyed Susan	*Rudbeckia*
Bladder Senna	*Colutea*
Blanket Flower	*Gaillardia*
Bleeding Heart	*Dicentra*
Bluebell	*Scilla*
Bottle Brush	*Callistemon*
Box	*Buxus*
Brompton Stock	*Matthiola*
Broom	*Cytisus*
Broom, Butcher's	*Ruscus*
Broom, Spanish	*Spartium*
Buckthorn, Sea	*Hippophae*
Bulrush	*Typha*
Bunny's Ears	*Stachys*
Butcher's Broom	*Ruscus*
Buttercup	*Ranunculus*
Calico Bush	*Kalmia*
Californian Poppy	*Eschscholzia*
Camomile	*Anthemis*
Campion	*Lychnis*
Candidum Lily	*Lilium*
Candytuft	*Iberis*
Canterbury Bell	*Campanula*
Cape Cowslip	*Lachenalia*
Cape Figwort	*Phygelius*
Cardinal Flower	*Lobelia*
Cardoon	*Cynara*
Carnation	*Dianthus*
Catmint	*Nepeta*
Cherry	*Prunus*
Cherry, Cornelian	*Cornus*
Cherry, Winter	*Solanum*
China Aster	*Callistephus*
Chincherinchee	*Ornithogalum*
Chinese Bell Flower	*Platycodon*
Chinese Lantern	*Physalis*
Christmas Rose	*Helleborus*
Clary	*Salvia*
Columbine	*Aquilegia*
Cone Flower	*Rudbeckia*
Convolvulus	*Ipomoea*

Coral Bells	*Heuchera*
Cornelian Cherry	*Cornus*
Cornflower	*Centaurea*
Cotton Thistle	*Onopordon*
Cowslip, Cape	*Lachenalia*
Cowslip, Jerusalem	*Pulmonaria*
Crab, Flowering	*Malus*
Crocus, Autumn	*Colchicum*
Crown Imperial	*Fritillaria*
Cup and Saucer Plant	*Cobaea*
Cupid's Dart	*Catananche*
Currant, Flowering	*Ribes*
Daffodil	*Narcissus*
Daisy, Barberton	*Gerbera*
Daisy, Michaelmas	*Aster*
Daisy, Shasta	*Chrysanthemum*
Day Lily	*Hemerocallis*
Dead Nettle	*Lamium*
Dogwood	*Cornus*
Edelweiss	*Leontopodium*
Elephant's Ears	*Bergenia*
Evening Primrose	*Oenothera*
Everlasting Flowers	*Helichrysum, Limonium*
Fennel	*Foeniculum*
Fern, Maidenhair	*Adiantum*
Fern, Royal	*Osmunda*
Figwort, Cape	*Phygelius*
Firethorn	*Pyracantha*
Flamingo Flower	*Anthurium*
Flax	*Linum*
Flax, New Zealand	*Phormium*
Fleabane	*Erigeron*
Flowering Currant	*Ribes*
Forget-me-not	*Myosotis*
Foxglove	*Digitalis*
Foxtail Lily	*Eremurus*
French Marigold	*Tagetes*
Gardener's Garters	*Phalaris*
Geranium	*Pelargonium*
Globe Flower	*Trollius*
Globe Thistle	*Echinops*
Glory of the Sun	*Leucocoryne*
Goat's Beard, False	*Astilbe*
Goat's Rue	*Galega*
Golden Rod	*Solidago*
Gorse, Spanish	*Genista*
Gourd	*Cucurbita*
Grape Hyacinth	*Muscari*
Guelder Rose	*Viburnum*
Guernsey Lily	*Nerine*
Gum Tree	*Eucalyptus*
Hawthorn	*Crataegus*
Hazel	*Corylus*
Heaths and Heather	*Erica*
Heliotrope, Winter	*Petasites*
Holly	*Ilex*
Holly, Sea	*Eryngium*
Hollyhock	*Althaea*
Honesty	*Lunaria*
Honeysuckle	*Lonicera*
Hop	*Humulus*
Hornbeam	*Carpinus*

Houseleek	*Sempervivum*
Hyacinth, Grape	*Muscari*
Hyacinth, Summer	*Galtonia*
Hyacinth, Wild	*Scilla*
Iceland Poppy	*Papaver*
Ivy	*Hedera*
Japonica	*Chaenomeles*
Jasmine	*Jasminum*
Jasmine, Madagascar	*Stephanotis*
Jerusalem Cowslip	*Pulmonaria*
Jerusalem Sage	*Phlomis*
Jonquil	*Narcissus*
Kaffir Lily	*Schizostylis*
Lady's Mantle	*Alchemilla*
Lamb's Ears	*Stachys*
Lamb's Tongue	*Stachys*
Larch	*Larix*
Larkspur	*Delphinium*
Laurel, Common	*Prunus*
Laurel, Spotted	*Aucuba*
Lavender	*Lavandula*
Lavender Cotton	*Santolina*
Lavender, Sea	*Limonium*
Leopard's Bane	*Doronicum*
Lilac	*Syringa*
Lily	*Lilium*
Lily, African	*Agapanthus*
Lily, Arum	*Zantedeschia*
Lily, Belladonna	*Amaryllis*
Lily, Candidum	*Lilium*
Lily, Day	*Hemerocallis*
Lily, Foxtail	*Eremurus*
Lily, Guernsey	*Nerine*
Lily, Kaffir	*Schizostylis*
Lily, Madonna	*Lilium*
Lily, Peruvian	*Alstroemeria*
Lily, Scarborough	*Vallota*
Lily, Snake's Head	*Fritillaria*
Lily, Tiger	*Lilium*
Lily, Torch	*Gloriosa*
Lily, Water	*Nymphaea*
Lily-of-the-Valley	*Convallaria*
Lily-of-the-Valley Tree	*Pieris*
Lime	*Tilia*
Lords and Ladies	*Zantedeschia*
Love-in-the-Mist	*Nigella*
Love-lies-bleeding	*Amaranthus*
Lupin	*Lupinus*
Madagascar Jasmine	*Stephanotis*
Madonna Lily	*Lilium*
Maidenhair Fern	*Adiantum*
Mallow	*Lavatera*
Maple	*Acer*
Marigold	*Calendula*
Marigold, African and French	*Tagetes*
May	*Crataegus*
Meadow Rue	*Thalictrum*
Mexican Orange Blossom	*Choisya*
Michaelmas Daisy	*Aster*
Mignonette	*Reseda*

Common Name	Botanical Name
Milk Thistle	*Silybum*
Mimosa	*Acacia*
Mistletoe	*Viscum*
Mock Orange	*Philadelphus*
Monkshood	*Aconitum*
Montbretia	*Tritonia*
Montbretia, Garden	*Crocosmia*
Morning Glory	*Ipomoea*
Mother-in-law's Tongue	*Sansevieria*
Mountain Ash	*Sorbus*
Mouse Plant	*Arisarum*
Mullein	*Verbascum*
Nasturtium	*Tropaeolum*
Nettle, Dead	*Lamium*
New Zealand Daisy Bush	*Olearia*
New Zealand Flax	*Phormium*
Obedient Plant	*Physostegia*
Opium Poppy	*Papaver*
Orach	*Atriplex*
Orchid, Poor Man's	*Schizanthus*
Pampas Grass	*Cortaderia*
Pasque Flower	*Pulsatilla*
Passion Flower	*Passiflora*
Peach	*Prunus*
Pendant Silver Lime	*Tilia*
Periwinkle	*Vinca*
Peruvian Lily	*Alstroemeria*
Pine	*Pinus*
Pineapple Flower	*Eucomis*
Pinks	*Dianthus*
Plum	*Prunus*
Plume Poppy	*Macleaya*
Poinsettia	*Euphorbia*
Poor Man's Orchid	*Schizanthus*
Poppy, Californian	*Eschscholzia*
Poppy, Iceland	*Papaver*
Poppy, Opium	*Papaver*
Poppy, Plume	*Macleaya*
Poppy, Shirley	*Papaver*
Pot Marigold	*Calendula*
Primrose, Evening	*Oenothera*
Privet	*Ligustrum*
Pussy Willow	*Salix*
Quaking Grass	*Briza*
Quince	*Chaenomeles*
Red Hot Poker	*Kniphofia*
Red Ink Plant	*Phytolacca*
Reed Mace	*Typha*
Rhubarb	*Rheum*
Ribbon Grass	*Phalaris*
Rose	*Rosa*
Rose, Christmas	*Helleborus*
Rose, Guelder	*Viburnum*
Rosemary	*Rosmarinus*
Rowan	*Sorbus*
Royal Fern	*Osmunda*
Rue	*Ruta*
Rue, Goat's	*Galega*
Rue, Meadow	*Thalictrum*
Russian Vine	*Polygonum*
Sage	*Salvia*
Sage, Jerusalem	*Phlomis*
St. John's Wort	*Hypericum*
Saxifrage, Giant	*Bergenia*
Scabious	*Scabiosa*
Scarborough Lily	*Vallota*
Scarlet Sage	*Salvia*
Sea Buckthorn	*Hippophae*
Sea Holly	*Eryngium*
Sea Lavender	*Limonium*
Shasta Daisy	*Chrysanthemum*
Shirley Poppy	*Papaver*
Smilax	*Asparagus*
Smoke Tree	*Rhus*
Snake's Head Lily	*Fritillaria*
Snapdragon	*Antirrhinum*
Snowball Tree	*Viburnum*
Snowberry	*Symphoricarpos*
Snowdrop	*Galanthus*
Snowdrop Tree	*Halesia*
Snowflake, Summer	*Leucojum*
Soldiers and Sailors	*Pulmonaria*
Solomon's Seal	*Polygonatum*
Southernwood	*Artemisia*
Spanish Broom	*Spartium*
Spanish Gorse	*Genista*
Spindle Tree	*Euonymus*
Spotted Laurel	*Aucuba*
Stag's Horn Sumach	*Rhus*
Star of Bethlehem	*Ornithogalum*
Statice	*Limonium*
Stock, Brompton	*Matthiola*
Stock, Virginia	*Malcolmia*
Strawberry Tree	*Arbutus*
Summer Hyacinth	*Galtonia*
Summer Snowflake	*Leucojum*
Sunflower	*Helianthus*
Sweet Pea	*Lathyrus*
Sweet Sultan	*Centaurea*
Sweet William	*Dianthus*
Teazle	*Dipsacus*
Thistle	*Onopordon*
Thistle, Globe	*Trollius*
Thistle, Milk	*Silybum*
Thorn Apple	*Datura*
Thrift	*Armeria*
Tiger Lily	*Lilium*
Toadflax	*Linaria*
Tobacco Plant	*Nicotiana*
Torch Lily	*Gloriosa*
True Lily	*Lilium*
Tuberose	*Polianthes*
Tulip	*Tulipa*
Turk's Cap	*Lilium*
Umbrella Plant	*Cyperus*
Valerian	*Kentranthus*
Vine	*Vitis*
Vine, Russian	*Polygonum*
Violet	*Viola*
Virginia Stock	*Malcolmia*
Wallflower	*Cheiranthus*
Wandering Jew	*Tradescantia*
Water Lily	*Nymphaea*
Wayfaring Tree	*Viburnum*
Whitebeam	*Sorbus*
Willow	*Salix*
Winter Aconite	*Eranthis*
Winter Cherry	*Solanum*
Winter Heliotrope	*Petasites*
Wintersweet	*Chimonanthus*
Witch Hazel	*Hamamelis*
Wormwood	*Artemisia*
Yarrow	*Achillea*
Yew	*Taxus*

BELOW Mimosa makes an attractive decoration but does not last well.

Index

INDEX

(Figures in italics refer to the captions)

W

Y Z

ACKNOWLEDGMENTS

My very grateful thanks go to Olive Middleton,
Fred Wilkinson and Rosemary Minter for
their help with the arrangements in this book.

The arrangements that
they did for me appear on
the following pages:

Olive Middleton
Page 22, 30, 39, 50, 51, 60, 61 (top), 66, 73 (bottom),
76 (bottom), 83 (bottom), 102 (bottom), 103 (bottom),
120, 122

Fred Wilkinson
Page 32, 48, 55, 62, 67 (top), 68,
70, 76 (top), 79, 88 (bottom), 90 (top), 95, 97,
104, 108, 109, 110 (left), 110 (right),
111, 121, 128, 129, 130, 131, 151, 153

Rosemary Minter
136, 137 (above), 142, 143

Photographs by **Malcolm Robertson**